PRAISE FOR
EMPOWER OUR GIRLS

"It's hard for me to decide if I like this book more as an educator, a mother, or for self-reflection. Every chapter gave me something to think about and will give the readers a challenge to carry into their lives in whatever role they occupy. Our girls are filled with so much worth and potential, and it is our moral imperative to help them find and share it. I love the 'Call to Action' because it is a takeaway I can implement immediately in my daily interactions with the wonderful girls in my life."

—Ramona Dunn,
principal

"*Empower Our Girls* is a powerful read. I savored every word and could not help but reflect on what my 'Call to Action' is now going to be. As a woman serving in a leadership capacity, I reflected on my journey, thought about the people in my life who shaped my thinking and being, and now feel compelled to do whatever it takes to pay it forward and support the empowerment of girls on their respective journeys. If you are looking to understand the *why* and *how* of lifting our girls up, you've found it. A hands-on approach to this topic is long overdue; thank you, Lyn and Adam, for shedding light while peeling back the layers to help us all–educators, parents, leaders, global citizens–recognize the importance of individually and collectively empowering our girls, for in doing so, we will undoubtedly impact generations not yet born."

—Onica Meyers,
committed lifelong learner

"Lynmara Colón and Adam Welcome have written a powerful narrative that is a must-read for all educators. Each chapter includes personal anecdotes and actionable ideas that readers can immediately implement in their own schools. This book inspires us to stand up for the girls in our lives by challenging the status quo and shifting the narrative to positively empower our future leaders."

—Heather Abney,
principal at Woodbridge Senior High School,
Prince William County Schools

"Rise Up. Overcome. Again and again. Lyn and Adam bring together many incredible educators, both men and women, who weave their own experiences into the message that our girls can be more. Through autobiographical experiences and a 'Call to Action,' *Empower Our Girls* will give anyone who has a young girl in his or her life a starting block to change the conversation. As a farmer's daughter myself, it would have been easy to fall into a homemaker role as many did before me . . . but I knew I wanted more. Now, as a mother and an elementary principal, I'm looking forward to using this book for inspiration as I raise my own daughter."

—Lindsy Stumpenhorst,
principal

"It doesn't matter if you are a teacher, principal, parent, or simply someone interested in making the world a better place–*Empower Our Girls* is a must-read that asks us to question the narratives surrounding females in the twenty-first century. A rising tide lifts all boats. When we empower our girls to be the best, most confident versions of themselves, everybody wins.

"Think of *Empower Our Girls* as an instructional manual on how to raise and educate powerful and self-assured women in the twenty-first century. The intensely personal stories in this book represent a choir of voices challenging us to question the perspectives, biases, and stereotypes we may unknowingly hold. Everyone—educators, administrators, and parents alike—can benefit from learning how to empower our girls to be the best, most confident versions of themselves."

—Nick Zefeldt,
county office instructional technology coordinator

"Adam and Lynmara are changing the narrative and embracing the power and potential of all girls. *Empower Our Girls* paints a relevant portrait of the current realities facing our young girls and encourages the reader to initiate conversations to challenge a stereotypical thought process, provide opportunities that may not be currently available, and empower girls to tear down walls and be the best versions of themselves. This book shares the powerful precept that, Yes, Girls Can!"

—Mandy Ellis,
wife, mother, elementary school principal,
author of *Lead with Literacy, Woman in Leadership*

"Colón and Welcome have offered readers fresh insight into the world girls face and the supports they need to rise and be their own success story. Modern days may have given rise to new issues for our girls to face, but the old adage is still the same: Girls can do it! Educators, parents, and communities must be intentional about encouraging girls to be their best and make no excuses for wanting to do it all! As a woman juggling a career, marriage, and children, I'm faced daily with thousands of decisions. It can be daunting, but I know I'm a success because I was never told, 'You can't do that.' I've been lucky in life to have a family, husband, friends, and colleagues that encourage me. Every girl should have this kind of support in her life. My three girls are my life's work, and I make sure they benefit from my experiences and encouragement. *Empower Our Girls* offers readers the tools to do the same for any girl in their lives!"

—Erin Hynes,
assistant superintendent

"This book is more than an awe-inspiring read about the strength inside powerful women; it is the beginning of a movement to do more than simply inspire our youth by empowering them for change! Lyn and Adam did an incredible job approaching the pathway to empowerment. I won't lie, 'Point beyond Physical Beauty' and 'Nudge Girls to Discover Their Voices' may be my favorite chapters in this book! I imagine this book will soon be a staple in any progressive teacher's library. People won't want to miss this next student-focused best seller!"

—Rae Hughart,
math teacher/director of training and development at Teach Better Team

"In *Empower Our Girls*, Lynmara Colón and Adam Welcome have written a celebration and a manifesto. They celebrate courageous girls and women who are finding their way in a world that is not always welcoming. We hear deeply and sometimes painfully personal stories and are reminded that there is much more work to be done before girls will reach their full potential. And therein lies the manifesto: the book is filled with calls to action, some simple and some seemingly impossible, and all meant to empower girls to embrace their own bodies and minds and make the world their own."

—Karen Richardson,
VSTE president, professor

"*Empower Our Girls* encourages us to reflect on our practice and helps us have the conversations we need to be having. I found myself either relating to or learning from each of the stories shared. I am so grateful my daughter is growing up in a world in which she is empowered."

—Diana Gill,
instructional technology coach and innovation specialist

"*Empower Our Girls* by Lynmara Colón and Adam Welcome celebrates the individuality of girls and inspires the adults in their lives to help them cultivate their natural power. As a society, we have a long way to go in the journey to gender equity. The information and calls to action shared in this book provide the reader with food for thought and strategies to help."

—Sarah Thomas, PhD,
founder of EduMatch

"*Empower Our Girls* by Lynmara Colón and Adam Welcome will spark much-needed conversations and action around equity and opportunity in our homes and schools. This text provides helpful reflection, emotional connection to the stories that are included, and specific action to promote and empower girls. Continued change is possible in our lifetime, and Lynmara and Adam remind us we can all make a difference."

—Sarah Johnson,
founder of In AWE, LLC, host of In AWE Podcast,
coauthor of *Balance Like a Pirate*, speaker, educator

"As a superintendent of a school system, I found *Empower Our Girls* very educational and eye opening, but as a *father* of a sixteen-year-old daughter, it was very convicting as I self-evaluated and realized that my expectations were not as high for my daughter as they were for my son. This is a must-read for those in school leadership who wish to truly 'empower' our girls."

—Rodney Kay,
superintendent

"Lynmara Colón and Adam Welcome fill a much-needed niche with a practical resource that provides a plethora of strategies on how to empower girls in the learning process. They write from the heart while leveraging their experience as teachers and administrators to inspire readers in their quest to help all girls unlock their potential."

—Eric Sheninger,
senior fellow, author, thought leader, innovator, educator, speaker

Empower Our Girls

Opening the Door for Girls to Achieve More

Lynmara Colón
Adam Welcome

Published by Dave Burgess Consulting, Inc.
San Diego, CA
daveburgessconsulting.com

Cover Design by Genesis Kohler
Editing and Interior Design by My Writers' Connection

Interior graphics adapted from original designs by Freepik

Library of Congress Control Number: 2019940276
Paperback ISBN: 978-1-949595-36-9
Ebook ISBN: 978-1-949595-37-6

First Printing: May 2019

From Adam

I dedicate this book to my wife Stacy, daughter Greta, my mother Maureen and mother-in-law Susan, as well as all the other strong and empowered females in my life who are getting after it and chasing their dreams. Thank you for your continued strength: It helps to guide me every single day.

From Lynmara

I dedicate this book to my father who ended every conversation between us letting me know how much he loved me. Dad, I hope that wherever you are, you are proud of the woman I've become. I also want to dedicate this book to my daughters Daniella and Gabriella. I am so proud and honored to be your mother. You both continue to amaze me. I hope you both grow up to be an inspiration to all the girls out there. This book is also for my mom, who showed me that no matter how difficult circumstances might seem, hard work pays off. And lastly, it's for the tribe of women who remind me on a daily basis that the past is just a stepping stone to the greatness that awaits. You all make every effort towards equality so worth it.

CONTENTS

FOREWORD

by Shelley Burgess

IF YOU ARE A woman of just about any age, you probably didn't give much thought as a child to how you and your girlfriends were treated differently from the boys your age. Maybe you were aware that society held certain expectations for girls and boys, but you grew up how you grew up. And if you're anything like me, you didn't think to question society's double standard; you didn't even know you *could* question it.

As a teenage girl in the 80s, *Seventeen* magazine was my go-to guide for knowing what and who I should aspire to be. Each month, my friends and I would pore over the latest issue. We would spend hours reading our horoscopes, trying the newest makeup techniques and beauty trends, and practicing the flirting tricks that promised "to capture that special guy's attention." And, of course, we would take all the quizzes that told us whether we talked too much, were too clingy, or needed to be more confident. *Seventeen* and other media like it set the standard for what was pretty enough, thin enough, fashionable enough, good enough, capable enough, or smart enough.

Awareness about gender inequality has increased dramatically since I was a young girl. We've seen women's empowerment movements gain momentum. We've cheered for the success some women have had in cracking that glass ceiling. And with all that progress, I would have hoped (and sort of assumed) that we as a society would be paying closer attention to the messages we are sending to our young girls about who they are, how they look, what makes them special, and what they can do and achieve.

With that hope in mind, I recently popped over to the *Seventeen* magazine website expecting to see something very different from the magazine I grew up reading. I felt certain I would find articles that pushed back on stereotypes and societal norms. I thought I would see stories that encouraged young girls to explore their passions and reach for their best. I hoped I would see pieces about women scientists, athletes, entrepreneurs, and engineers.

Instead I found these headlines:

"10 Major Signs You're Really in Love"

"Shawn Mendes Sent His Used Underwear to a Fan, and
I've Never Been So Jealous of Anyone in My Life"

"How to Get Rid of a Pimple"

"Do Hickeys Hurt?"

And these were the quizzes:

"Which Disney Princess Are You?"

"Does Your Crush Like You as More Than a Friend?
AKA the Most Frustrating Mystery of ALL Time."

"How to Become a Good Girlfriend"

"How Well Do You Know Taylor Swift's Boyfriends?"

"Who's Your One Direction Love Match?"

With the exception of the addition of an LGBTQ tab, I was disheartened at the minimal change in the messages that continue to bombard our young girls. They are constantly told that they are (and should be) measured by their appearance and their success as girlfriends (or worse, princesses). Add in the growing influence of social media, and these persistent messages are almost impossible to escape. Societal pressures to conform to other people's perceptions of what they *should* be continue to keep girls from even imagining all they *could* be.

I can clearly remember the first time I realized people had certain expectations of me because of my gender. I was seventeen years old and had just received my acceptance letter to attend UCLA. I felt capable and confident and ready to conquer the world. I eagerly shared the good news with my grandparents. My grandfather gave me a hug and said something like, "That's nice, but you shouldn't bother going to college." What I really needed, he told me, was to find a nice man to take care of me and raise a good family. For high school graduation, my grandparents gave me a set of silverware complete with steak knives, serving utensils, and a gravy ladle. It all came in a pretty wooden box with a note telling me it was something I could put in my "Hope Chest."

Similar expectations revealed themselves again when my boss reminded me that, as a young adult, being a woman meant things were different for me. Having successfully proven myself in an administrative role in my school district's office, I wanted to move into a site administration role where I could work more closely with teachers and students. I scheduled a conversation with my superintendent and shared with him my aspirations to be an assistant principal. He smiled kindly and said that every time he asked a principal whom they would like to have as an assistant principal, I was always one of three top candidates. (*Great!*) He went on to tell me, however, that the timing wasn't right because what was most important at that point in my life was that I "care for my family." (I was visibly pregnant at the time.) He assured me that once I'd had my baby and taken some time off, we could revisit the conversation about the next steps for my career. (*What?!*)

A few weeks later, I applied for a principalship in a neighboring district, got the job, and hopefully left that superintendent shaking his head.

As a forty-eight-year-old successful female leader, best-selling author, speaker, business owner, wife, and mother of two teenagers, I have been called "bitch" when I have held people accountable, "arrogant" when I have demonstrated confidence, "emotional" when I just needed to shed a few tears after finishing another sixteen-hour work day without seeing my kids, "cold" when I haven't been emotional or nurturing enough, and "hysterical" when I just needed to vent. And despite my proven track record and confidence in my abilities, I can *still* struggle with things like body image, fret over pictures of me posted on social media (especially since I have gained weight), question my ability to be a good mother, and wonder if I am doing enough and doing it all well enough.

Nothing that I read in *Seventeen* as a girl prepared me for the realities of being a successful woman. And despite all our progress, the messages our girls are getting today from popular magazines and social media haven't changed much. Neither have the stereotypical and prejudice-laden practices regarding women in the workplace. It's long-past time for those messages to change and those stereotypes to end.

In *Empower Our Girls: Opening the Door for Girls to Achieve More*, Adam and Lyn call on us—moms, dads, aunts, uncles, grandparents, teachers, principals, human beings—to say, "enough is enough." They encourage us to examine our practices, our rules, our procedures, our behaviors, and our language to determine if we are doing our part to help eradicate the gender bias that exists in our society and our schools. They also point out things we may be doing, even if unintentionally, that are contributing to the pressures and preconceptions that prevent girls from reaching for their full potential. And then they challenge us to take action, *right now.*

The authors have invited several women (along with a few men) to share their stories and perspectives on how we can be intentional about shifting the conversation. Some of what you read may surprise you and make you wonder how such outdated and irrational thinking could persist in our modern society. Other stories will inspire you to find ways to challenge girls to break down the perceived barriers that have been built by those messages they hear so often.

If a girl *wants* to raise a family as a stay-at-home mom, the message in *Empower Our Girls* is that she should have that freedom, without judgment. And if a girl *wants* to be an astronaut, a business owner, an engineer, or a coding-writing master, she should be encouraged to pursue those avenues as well, regardless of whether she also wants to have a family.

The point is, there are no limits to what girls can accomplish, and it's our job to make sure they know that. It's our job to *Empower Our Girls.*

INTRODUCTION

From Lynmara

As a young minority girl born and raised in Puerto Rico, I experienced a rough start filled with confusion and a lack of choices. I came from humble beginnings. My mother was a high school teacher, and my father was an auto mechanic. They taught me to keep a clean house and expect a big family. My mother often relied on my grandparents and neighbors to care for my sister and me while she juggled the demands of being a teacher and a mother. Watching her often left me dreaming of a better future and with a desire to remove roadblocks for my family once I grew up.

While I am proud of my background and the lessons I have learned, I knew a big family and a clean house weren't enough for me. These weren't wrong, but I wanted more. I wanted to go to school, pursue a career, and have an impact. Seeing the struggles of so many back home made me visualize what it could look like to become a leader, break the cycle of poverty, and be an agent of change for a town where options were often limited. I dreamed of leaving a legacy and showing others that no matter where you come from, we can all make a difference.

My grandmother understood. She saw my passion and desire, but she also knew firsthand that changing others' perceptions about a "woman's place" would be hard in our very conservative country. Every week we would have conversations about this while cooking and cleaning the house. Now as an adult, I appreciate the "sweet" balance she provided between being empowered to dream big things and being prepared for what traditionally my culture expected of me. Grandmother often told me stories about the challenges of caring for her children *and* working as a school custodian. I heard her passion and pride about her work, and I asked her questions about how much she was paid and about any opportunities for growth she might have had within her career. To her, they might simply have been stories; to me, they were a call to aspire for more.

My options didn't improve much by high school, and graduating at fifteen years old only seemed to limit them. I was perceived as just the "quiet, smart girl." In fact, the more I tried to speak up, the more I was questioned about my abilities. And I was not alone; some of my classmates were also afraid to share their opinions and stand up for what they believed was right. Training girls to be silent and agree with others was the norm from early in my childhood. If a girl challenged someone's thinking, she ran the risk of being perceived as conflictive or disruptive—definitely not "feminine" traits.

Every little girl dreams of being a mom—at least this is the message I got when I was growing up. From an early age, I was gifted with dolls and learned about diapers and bottles. I was raised to admire Barbie and dream of a "Prince Charming" who would provide protection and care for our children and me. Again, I know I was not alone. Having a family still seems *expected* of girls, many of whom are trained to be domestic CEOs. They pretend play with other girls in an attempt to perfect the art of being a mom and taking care of a house. And having a family seals the deal: The world then knows they have achieved success!

But what are girls to do when life doesn't go as planned? Nobody has mentored them for the unexpected. I never rehearsed what to do if children were not part of my equation, and my heart was destroyed when I learned having children would be impossible without medical assistance. Because the world puts so much value on women becoming moms, I suddenly lost confidence when I found out this was not possible for me. I felt a sense of shame and devastation when I was faced with the news. Perhaps it would have been more bearable if I had known from an early age that my value did not come only from motherhood, but I was left trying to understand a situation pretend play had not prepared me for.

As a result, when I was gifted with twin girls, I knew helping them become strong and confident young ladies was my only option. My mission has been to teach them that value and worth do not come from others but rather from the work they do within themselves. I hope this book empowers girls to understand that tears and vulnerability are not signs of weakness and to assure them they have a seat at the right table where their ideas can and will be heard.

We are writing this book out of a sense of responsibility to push our girls to be the best they can be. Our goal is to highlight role models who will assure them they can do more, no matter where they come from. Adam and I want to open the door to a world of possibilities where our girls get to experience the life they deserve.

From Adam

My first-grade daughter, Greta, has already started:

Why are there so many shirts and signs about girl power? How come boys don't wear those kinds of shirts?

Well, girls don't always have the same opportunities as boys, unfortunately.

That's not fair! We need to do something about it, Dad!

Yes—yes we do!

That might sound like an exaggeration, but unfortunately, the evidence is clear:

- Sixty-six percent of fourth-grade girls say they like science and math, but only eighteen percent of all college engineering majors are female.
- In the 1980s women made up thirty-five percent of computer science graduates in the United States. Today the number is seventeen percent.
- Women make up eleven percent of Fortune 500 executives.
- Only five percent of tech start-ups are owned by women.
- Women represent thirty-three percent of judges in United States courts.

- Ambitious girls are often perceived as pushy and selfish.
- Crying is viewed as a weakness instead of a powerful demonstration of emotion and humanity.

At Google women make up thirty percent of the company's overall workforce but hold only seventeen percent of the company's tech jobs. At Facebook fifteen percent of tech roles are staffed by women, and at Twitter it's only ten percent.

Lynmara and I believe it's time for these numbers and situations to change. Far too many girls and women don't achieve their full potential because they've been told:

- No.
- Stand to the side.
- That's a boy's job.
- You don't want to get dirty.

Or they've gotten the message they should stay on the sidelines and be quiet. If they try to take charge, they're "bossy," while a young boy demonstrating the same behavior is considered a leader. This needs to change. Our girls deserve the same opportunities boys have.

In this book, you'll find stories about women. Some of them are personal stories. Some of them are written by men about their daughters or other women in their lives. Some are stories of how women were held back at times, how they persevered, and what they did to move forward. Others are stories of what they would do differently if they could go back in time.

Our hope is that this book inspires you to stand up for the girls in your life. Whether you're a teacher, a parent, a coach, an aunt or uncle, or a grandmother or grandfather, empower your girls to hear a different narrative. Change the conversation—for *them*.

THE
POWER
OF
ROLE
MODELS

CHAPTER 1

Provide Relevant Role Models

CAREER FAIRS ARE COMMON events in our schools. Students look forward to them, and parents often volunteer at them. Community members come and share with students why their jobs are fulfilling, inspiring students to dream about serving in their role. Unfortunately, most career fairs seem to lack female leaders, thereby denying girls the opportunity to see how women are taking on roles often filled by males.

During a recent career fair at our school, I (Lynmara) noticed men spoke for all the jobs related to safety and security (police officers, military personnel, and firefighters). While the kids were excited to try on gear and ask questions about the presenters' adventures, I kept wondering if our girls could relate. Women have been serving in the military since the Revolutionary War;

however, the number continues to be low for those serving on active duty (just fourteen percent in the Army). I wonder if our girls understand they can choose to protect our country and be successful doing it. I would be interested to see the toy industry create dolls representing women in these fields.

A visit to technical schools across the country reveals, not surprisingly, that most students in the auto shop, electricity, and computer science programs are male. Our girls need female role models in these areas from an early age, so they are not perceived as "different" or "tomboys" if they choose these career paths. Girls deserve to see women making a difference in jobs previously filled predominantly by men.

> During a recent career fair at our school, I (Lynmara) noticed men spoke for all the jobs related to safety and security . . . I kept wondering if our girls could relate.

As children, my brother and I spent a lot of time with my father in his auto shop. While my dad involved my brother in his work with the cars, he sent me to the parts warehouse to do inventory. Dad expected my brother would follow in his steps (which he did), but where was I left? You guessed right—counting parts! My dad did not think automotive mechanic jobs were for girls. Whenever I tried to step foot outside the warehouse, he said the same things: *Go away; I do not want you to get dirty* or *This area is for the guys; you can get hurt.* So even though I learned the names and functions of the auto parts, I never got any hands-on training with them. I missed the most important aspect of auto mechanics: the practice.

Every girl should be taught the basic anatomy of a car and how to change a tire, so she will be prepared in case of an emergency and avoid having to pay more to fix her car. Knowing the number for your insurance company is great, but being a proactive girl in these situations is *powerful*. In order to achieve this sense of power, girls need to have female role models to learn these skills from. They should have access to strong female role models who can answer questions, provide encouragement, and share with them the message that they are not alone.

Our school libraries are a great option for giving girls access to female role models; however, during a recent inventory of our library, I noticed a lack of books with female heroines. While we had biographies and historical fiction books with female leading characters, we had few fiction books with female heroines. I had never looked at our library inventory this way. As a principal, I feel responsible for providing girls with access to books at an early age, but what if these books do not represent everything a girl can be? I applaud authors like Andrea Beaty for writing stories about girls who are scientists and engineers and changing the traditional narrative that implies only men are good at these careers. Schools must build libraries that give students a wide variety of books with characters they can *all* relate to.

Michelle Obama knows these challenges well. While in high school, she had to drive one and a half hours to get to the magnet school she attended because there was no magnet school closer to her. Later when she applied to Princeton, she was told she was "not good enough" because she was a female aspiring to enter a male-dominated field. I can't help but think about what would have happened if she had not pushed herself to be the best she could be, staying focused on the words of her parents who encouraged her to stand strong despite rejections. What would have happened if she had taken *no* for an answer? Not only did she overcome her challenges and graduate from Harvard, but twenty years later, she also became the First Lady of our country! Coming from a working-class family and focusing on the high expectations she had for herself, Michelle Obama achieved her dream of receiving an education and making an impact on the lives of others. Because she has been vulnerable with the public about the challenges of balancing her priorities while fulfilling her dream, she is a great example to girls that even women in positions of power have to persevere. Girls are entitled to have access to role models like Michelle Obama, amazing women who not only have made significant accomplishments but also have overcome great challenges to do so.

Girls are watching everything adults do. They learn about equality and define their choices based on the things they see and perceive from adults. Our girls need strong female role models to admire, role models who will influence and inspire them to take risks. Be the role model who leaves a legacy for them to follow. Your girls deserve it!

A CALL TO ACTION

★ Organize an event where female role models speak to girls.

★ Set up coaching sessions with diverse role models for girls.

★ Schedule time to meet with girls who can benefit from listening to your story.

CHAPTER 2

Share Your Past to Impact the Future

From Amber Heffner, ICE Executive Director

GROWING UP AS A female, I often wondered, "What would it be like to experience life as a male?" Why did I ask this? Was it because I felt I had to work harder to be seen equally? Did I think I'd have a better life or a better story if I were a male? As I reflected on my own journey and considered all the people who had influenced me and the experiences I'd had, I realized I had a story I could share to help others. Girls and women need to celebrate their stories and share their journeys! Women cannot make changes and impact the trajectory of a climate without building empathy and understanding through sharing their stories.

My story was formed in part by the female role models making significant impacts in society as I was growing up. For example, Edith Green, U.S. Representative from Oregon, co-sponsored Title IX, which allowed enrollment of women in athletics programs and professional schools. I was a young athlete at the time, and I can still remember buying my first pair of high tops from the men's department since high tops weren't yet made for women. I remember watching my P.E. teacher count the number of pull-ups the boys did and then insisting I have the same opportunity. (And yes, I always did at least one more pull-up than the boy with the highest number!)

> **Girls and women need to celebrate their stories and share their journeys!**

In 1981 Sandra Day O'Connor became the first woman appointed to the U.S. Supreme Court. I took every opportunity available in school to research and write about this major milestone. In 1983 Dr. Sally K. Ride became the first American woman to travel into space, and in 1984 Geraldine Ferraro became the first woman to be nominated for vice president on a major party ticket.

I was also fortunate to have had strong female role models in my personal life. My mom raised four daughters while working alongside my dad in the family business and on the farm. She never shied away from "man's" work. In fact, because my parents modeled this so well, I grew up not knowing there were different expectations for what men and women could do. To me, they were the same.

My grandma was also a strong female role model. She was a determined woman who attended college and received her degree in music education in the early 1940s. She was a living example of elegance, determination, and success. Although she majored in education, her true calling was business. In the early 1960s, after starting a family, my grandparents had the opportunity to purchase a grain elevator and begin a forty-plus-year family business. Being part of a family-owned business and seeing my grandma succeed as a professional businesswoman taught me the importance of customer service, hard work, servant leadership, and always finding the positive.

So many women *and* men influenced my journey by:

- Supporting me throughout my education;
- Teaching me women can be good leaders;
- Mentoring me as I entered the workforce;
- Dedicating time to share their story with me and listen to mine;
- Seeing the strength and talents I had as an individual; and
- Encouraging me to do what I wanted to do.

I now have an adult daughter, and while I know the challenges she faced growing up, I also see the strength she gained from those challenges serving her well as she continues to succeed. I'm excited to know part of her success has come from the influence of so many strong female role models before her, women who are doing for her what others did for me: sharing their stories, listening to her, encouraging her, letting her be who she is, and letting her enjoy football while also singing and dancing in a pretty white dress.

I encourage you to reflect on the impact your role models have had on your life and consider your influence on others. As educators and leaders, you have helped break a lot of barriers for girls, but there is still more work to do. Sharing your stories can inspire and encourage the girls in your lives to be all they can be and help you leave your own impact on the future.

A CALL TO ACTION

★ How can your story help young girls think about their future in a different way?

★ What qualities or experiences as a child had a positive impact on you as an adult?

CHAPTER 3

Provide a Tribe of Mentors

SUCCESSFUL EXECUTIVES AND LEADERS all have something in common: a mentor. A mentor is not a best friend or a *yes* person, but instead someone who provides support, wisdom, and advice on an ongoing basis. Having both female and male mentors can help girls build confidence and realize they too can make great contributions to any field or community. More than ever, young girls need support to craft goals and find ways to achieve them. We have spoken to a significant number of female leaders who have shared with us the important role mentors have played in their lives.

Mentors can build up young girls in a number of ways, from coaching them during their search for a promotion, to helping them navigate difficult times, serving as a sounding board, or sharing experiences with similar challenges. If you know that every successful woman has a group of people who are behind her and cheering for her, then why not be proactive and invest in girls by giving them that same kind of support? How powerful girls would be if they had a tribe of mentors rallying around them and cheering them on whether they win or lose.

I (Lynmara) did not have this support as a child. Raised in a single-mother home, all my experience centered on how difficult life would be if *I* became a single mother. My mother did an amazing job sheltering my sister and me from what I now know was a challenging time balancing motherhood, a career, and trying to make it on her own. My father was involved in my life, but I didn't have professional support to assist me through the challenges I experienced when my parents got divorced. I did not have access to books or therapy for support during a time I now realize can be life-changing for any child. I simply reached out to friends who shared their experiences and frustrations about complicated schedules, two-family holidays, and parents arguing over child support.

> Mentors can be either men or women, and they should be trusted individuals who are there to build girls up, not tear them down.

As a principal, I knew I had to change this for my students. I became very intentional about talking with parents who were going through a divorce and telling them how important mentors were for their children. While I believe therapy can be key to a child's healing, a mentor can provide additional help by listening to and also building up a child. Their focus is not on fixing the issue but rather on providing some skills to cope with it. I have seen mentor relationships change students *and* adults.

As a minority female, I have faced many challenges since I moved to the United States; however, I have found a few mentors who have encouraged me, given me advice, and also reined me in when I was getting ahead of myself. I truly believe my mentors have been key to my professional success; without them, I would have made irrational decisions. My mentors have helped me navigate the path of leadership every step of the way.

With all the distractions and challenges our girls face, having someone to provide a different perspective can help them become stronger. At school, girls should have access to mentors and be able to get feedback on leadership. They should have a trusted adult who can give them feedback after a presentation, speech, or game. Unfortunately, girls have learned that asking for feedback is a sign of weakness and gives the perception of lacking confidence or being insecure. We have to show them that this simply is not true by helping them see the benefits of having a tribe of mentors. Mentors can be either men or women, and they should be trusted individuals who are there to build girls up, not tear them down.

I had the opportunity recently to hear Kim Lair speak about the unique characteristics of each generation of life. As she described how these characteristics show up in the workplace, I could not help but think how valuable it would be for girls to have a mentor as they navigate every stage of life. Each mentor would offer different perspectives and advice related to the unique issues of their particular generation. The role of women in the workplace and other areas has evolved. Mentors who can tell girls stories and give them first-hand information about the wins women have had over the years can be a powerful influence on girls as they continue to pursue careers and roles that women in the past could only dream about having.

A CALL TO ACTION

★ Contact a local school or non-profit about serving as a mentor for a girl or woman.

★ Reflect on the advice you offer female colleagues. How does it inspire growth?

★ Advocate for having more female speakers at conferences and workshops.

CHAPTER 4

Expectations and Exposure

LET'S TALK ABOUT EXPECTATIONS for a minute. This message is for moms *and* dads; it's not just a female issue. Males—especially dads—are involved in a major way.

What expectations do you have for your daughter? What do you want her to be? Where do you want her to go? How do you want her to be treated in society—currently and when she's an adult? Have you thought about the differences between her childhood and your own?

I (Adam) am not sure you talk about this enough or think about what you actually expect for your daughters. I get it. You're busy with school, outside activities, work, and keeping up with daily schedules. But your daughter's future is too important to brush off and not focus on. Girls are at a societal disadvantage right out of the gate in many areas of their lives. It's imperative the adults in their lives have extremely high expectations. But it's even more important to foster and grow them.

While some girls may surpass the expectations, many may not because they don't realize they *can*. All they know is the original expectation. Girls need to be pushed and encouraged by the adults in their lives. They need to see strong and passionate women they can look up to and emulate. How are you creating opportunities for girls to see and be mentored by strong women across a multitude of sectors within society?

Mentors don't need to be famous. Someone just a few years older is a great person to start with. I believe you can turn an older girl into a mentor of sorts without her even knowing it. For example, you can watch a sporting event with your daughter at a local college or high school and follow a player throughout the game or competition. Then you can talk to your daughter at home during dinner—or during another teachable moment—about what you saw and heard about the player and encourage your daughter that she can do the same some-day. Maybe your daughter will even get the courage to talk with the player after a game sometime. The most important thing is for girls to realize this mentor is just a person a little ahead of them in life and understand they have the ability to do and be the same as their mentor. When girls can see someone else in action, they start to believe it's possible for them to achieve their goals as well.

> ## How are you creating opportunities for girls to see and be mentored by strong women across a multitude of sectors within society?

My wife and I recently took our daughter, Greta, and her friend to a local college and watched the women's soccer team compete. For a full week before the game, she talked about how excited she was. Because of all the buildup to the game, Greta had a glow in her eye as we entered the stadium. She checked the roster and pointed to different players on the field during warm-ups. She knew they were from all across the country and even from some other coun-tries as well. I could see her brain expanding with possibilities as she watched them. Seeing a female soccer player on the field who was older, confident, and athletic gave my daughter and her friend a view into who they could someday be. This was powerful.

Our family also reads picture books or appropriate non-fiction books about famous and strong women throughout history. Because Greta has been infatuated with Pocahontas since she was in kindergarten, my wife and I have done research with her about Pocahontas and read to her from books beyond her reading level to encourage her love for this historical figure and all she stood for. This is super simple and a great way to inspire and motivate our daughter by helping her learn about a strong female figure. When Greta was in first grade, she checked out the only two books about Pocahontas in her school library no less than twenty times. She was mesmerized by this powerful, historical, *female* figure.

Reading "beyond" a book can also be beneficial. My kindergarten son recently came home with a rather large non-fiction book called *The Greatest Moments in Sports,* full of stories about football and basketball games, the Olympics, and other sporting events. A few days later, Greta picked up the book, and what she pointed out made me so proud. I knew exactly what she was going to say: "Dad, there are twenty-five stories in this book about great moments in sports, and there are only three about women. What's up with that?"

I beamed with pride, not because she found fault with the book but because she was looking beyond what the author concluded and knew there had to be more. In reality, this book included only one person's opinion about the greatest moments in sports; however, it was also a *New York Times* Best Seller, so a lot of people read the message.

While this could have been the end of our conversation, instead we started researching other amazing female athletes and *their* great moments in sports. We researched, watched YouTube videos, and checked current athletes' Instagram pages to see what they had recently accomplished. And then we wrote our own ending for the book. *The Greatest Moments in Sports* was published over fifteen years ago. Since then many more women have achieved their own greatest moments:

- In 2012 the U.S. women's soccer team won gold at the Olympics;
- Mo'Ne Davis became the first female pitcher to win the Little League World Series;
- Misty May-Treanor and Kerri Walsh received multiple wins and medals for beach volleyball;
- Missy Franklin won four gold medals in two days at the 2012 Olympics;

- Serena and Venus Williams co-ranked as the #1 players in both singles and doubles tennis;
- In 2012, for the first time in Olympic history, every country in the world had female representation; and
- In 2008 Danica Patrick won the Indy Japan 300, making her the first female to win an Indy race.

Don't let what *you* see or read dictate the story your girls hear. Sometimes you may need to dig to find what you're looking for and also what they need! Consider the books in your school libraries. If the literature accessible to girls in your school doesn't include an appropriate representation of other females throughout history who did amazing things—or who were given a voice in general—look for other books and make them available to them. Our girls deserve the opportunity to read about the women who came before them and learn about their accomplishments right alongside those of their male counterparts.

A CALL TO ACTION

★ Are there events happening in your neighborhood where you could take your girls to see potential female mentors?

★ Look at the books you read with your girls or the ones they're reading. What's missing from the storyline? How are the female characters presented?

THE POWER OF OPPORTUNITY

CHAPTER 5

Take a Chance on Them

✳ *From Courtney Orzel, superintendent*

YOU DON'T LOOK LIKE a school superintendent.

I hear this often. While I'm not sure what a superintendent is supposed to look like to the general public, I hear this enough to know they don't think I'm it. I'm okay with this. I never planned to be a school superintendent. I wanted to be a teacher. Perhaps I'm dating myself, but lining up and teaching my Cabbage Patch Kids was my favorite playtime as a kid. In fact, teaching is all I ever wanted to do. But some strong women saw something in me and paved the way for me to have a career I never dreamed of.

When I finished student teaching in the middle of the semester, no teaching jobs were available, so I became a recruiter for engineers. While I enjoyed the people, I despised the work. In six months, I earned triple the amount of money I would make as a teacher in one year, but I couldn't wait to leave this job and get a teaching position.

I started my teaching career when a principal took a chance on me and hired me as a middle-school language arts and reading teacher. I felt I had finally made it; however, they also wanted me to start a drama program. I had *no* experience with theater beyond my student teaching experience, but when my principal asked me to start the new program, of course I said, "Sure, I can do that!"

Three years later, I applied for a high school English position even though I did not have the exact qualifications required; however, I got an interview, and it turned out to be for a position teaching English, speech—*and* theater! I would need to create my own curricula for the courses *and* teach *five* different classes every year. *And* I would be the drama director. Again, I didn't have the specific experience needed, but when I was offered the job, I said, "Sure, I can do that!"

> ✳ **Ambition and taking initiative are more important than knowing how to do every single part of the job.** ✳

When a new graduate school cohort began, my supervisor asked me to consider taking courses toward a master's degree in administration. Since I had nothing else to do but direct shows until 10:00 every evening—on top of all my other teaching responsibilities—I said, "Sure, I can do that!" When presented with a new opportunity, it's always best to jump in with both feet!

The month I completed my degree, I was encouraged to apply for a Dean of Students job posted for a middle school. Even though I wasn't qualified for the job, I applied because it looked like a great opportunity. Someone else took another chance on me, and I got the job.

Two years later, my title changed from Dean to Assistant Principal. When a principal position opened up, I was encouraged to apply and met with the superintendent. Yet again, I had no experience, but I liked the superintendent and the district, and I liked the challenge. Thankfully, she took a chance on me. In fact, if it weren't for her vision, inspiration, and encouragement,

I wouldn't be where I am today professionally. For the next nine years, I served as a middle school principal. When this superintendent retired, I was appointed to take her place.

Job requirements or preferred qualifications—like five years of teaching experience *required* or five years of successful administrative experience *preferred*—never stopped me from applying. If I liked the opportunity, I applied for it. If I had been deterred by job "requirements" (and if the people in charge of hiring hadn't taken a chance on me), I wouldn't be where I am today.

Through my experience, I learned I didn't have to be the most knowledgeable person to take on a new role or challenge. I could learn and grow as I went along. Sometimes taking the chance is all that's required to see results. Ambition and taking initiative are more important than knowing how to do every single part of the job.

I also learned from some amazing mentors. Adam Welcome inspired me to start a blog, begin vlogging, and write a chapter for this book. He also encouraged me to get active on social media and expand my network. You can do the same. Expand your network and find your own amazing mentors.

Finally, take a chance on others and give them opportunities. If you see something in them they can't quite see yet, point out their talents and encourage them to try. Telling someone what you see in them might be just what they need to spark their passion and be inspired to take a risk and shine. Girls deserve to be empowered in every possible opportunity. If they have an interest in a position they're technically not qualified for, they should just go for it, just *try*. What's the worst that can happen? They don't get the job? They definitely won't get the job if they don't try. And they will learn more about themselves in the *trying*, regardless of what the outcome is. Encourage girls that they *can* do this!

A CALL TO ACTION

★ What can you do to encourage girls to change their narrative and embrace opportunities?

★ What can you do to help the girls you know aim higher in their goals and aspirations?

CHAPTER
6

Push Them to Achieve More

MY (ADAM) WIFE, STACY, is a practitioner of medicine—a very successful physician's assistant in an emergency department. While she is extremely happy with what she's doing, we've had many conversations about why she got her license to practice as a PA instead of going to medical school to become a physician. Stacy is happy with who she is as a person, so confidence wasn't the issue. Her decision was more about the opportunity. Stacy didn't have any female role models who were physicians, and the role models she had weren't encouraging her to become a doctor or even telling her she *could* become a doctor. If she'd known this opportunity was available to her, she might have made a different choice.

When our girls see other females doing what they dream of doing personally or fulfilling roles they haven't even considered before, they're going to have a higher degree of confidence that they can do these things themselves. Be proactive to plant seeds in girls' minds about what's possible for them! For example, a statement as simple as "I'm really proud you want to become a teacher. You exhibit great leadership skills and should think about getting into administration someday!" can change the trajectory of a girl's life if planted at the right time, by the right person, with the right degree of enthusiasm, and repeated regularly. Girls deserve to be aware of all their opportunities to achieve—opportunities to do *more* with their lives—and be encouraged to pursue them.

But some may say not all kids should be pushed to achieve more. After I spoke at a school district conference, one teacher in the audience disagreed with me about all kids having the opportunity to go to college and do more with their lives. At first I didn't believe what he was saying, but he repeated himself:

Some kids are just going to grow up to mow lawns. We need people to do this. Why should we want more for those kids?

Certainly, some of our kids may grow up to mow lawns, but shouldn't we at least expose them to something more? We're not making students follow a certain path; we're simply highlighting their opportunity to do so.

I feel very deeply that our girls should have the opportunity to do more, be more, see more, learn more, and reach their full potential. Not everyone will grow up to be a physician, own their own company, or play a professional sport. But if adults can highlight opportunities for girls, then they may have the ability to achieve something better for themselves, and they deserve this opportunity!

> **We're not making students follow a certain path; we're simply highlighting their opportunity to do so.**

As a minority female, I (Lynmara) experienced firsthand how others expected less of me because of where I came from. During high school, I was only invited to attend career fairs focused on certain careers. I was not exposed to any science or engineering opportunities. My teachers assumed I was not interested in or capable of serving in those roles. Not until my first year of college did I learn of the numerous opportunities available for women in the areas of leadership and technology. This misrepresentation robbed me of the opportunity to learn about other careers at an earlier age.

This is one of the main reasons I feel strongly about having diverse representation during career fairs and encouraging girls to learn about jobs they are afraid to consider pursuing. In a world where things are changing so fast and creativity is a must, adult leaders cannot afford to put kids in boxes and assume they do not have the potential to do more. Get out of the way and let them show you how far they can go. Help them set their sights high, be bold in their choices, and dream big. Highlight all possible opportunities and give them the chance to end up exactly where they want to be.

A CALL TO ACTION

★ How can you increase the opportunities for the girls in your life?

★ Show girls a variety of career opportunities and highlight the options they hold.

CHAPTER 7

Recruit Them

SOMETIMES GIRLS MAY NEED a personal invitation from a teacher, parent, or trusted mentor to let them know it's safe or acceptable to participate in certain activities. In many cases, that may be the deciding factor between them participating or opting to watch from the sidelines and never having the experience. As a new principal, I (Adam) wanted to start a coding club on campus and was beyond excited to get it off the ground. After sharing a Google Form with all 560 families from our school, I waited for kids to sign up. Within the first couple of days, over twenty students were interested in joining the club! I eventually had to cap participation at twenty-five for the initial round.

As I looked over the spreadsheet to see who had signed up, I was quickly hit in the face with an unfortunate reality. Of the twenty-five kids who had signed up, only *two* were girls. Why were only eight percent of the participants girls? I was frustrated.

I immediately thought of my own daughter, Greta. While she was only three years old at the time, I wondered if she would have signed up for a class like this if she were older. Would she have been encouraged to sign up? Would she have felt safe learning to code from her male principal? How would she feel in the first class when only one other girl was in attendance? Would she come back for the second class? What would her coding future look like if she didn't see more females in class or have the ability to learn coding from another female?

> As other girls saw their female friends coding and talking about their experiences, they wanted to join the class also.

I realized we had work to do in this area, and the only thing I could do immediately was *recruit* girls for the class, so I did! I texted parents of girls I thought would enjoy the class and encouraged them to sign up their daughters. I went to lunch recess and recruited more girls who I thought would be interested and signed them up. Accepting only eight percent wasn't an option. As a school, we had to do better, and we did! As other girls saw their female friends coding and talking about their experiences, they wanted to join the class also, and we went from twenty-five students to over thirty-five in the class!

It's just not acceptable to have that big of a gender discrepancy in your numbers and not just in a coding class. When you build a culture of gender equality, with recruiting or not, it sends a message to the entire community that what you're striving for is important, and you're not going to settle for anything less.

Educators, parents, and friends, if your girls don't initiate their own participation in areas where their interests and talents can be developed, your job is to recruit them. Point out their talents, pair them with opportunities, and encourage them to be all they can be!

A CALL TO ACTION

★ If your local school does not currently offer coding classes, encourage educators to make them available for girls.

★ Volunteer to teach coding classes in your area. Visit code.org for more information.

CHAPTER 8

Teach Them to Seize Opportunities

⭐ From Erin Jones, educator and speaker ⭐

LITTLE DID I KNOW my love for basketball would open the door to so many amazing opportunities.

As a young woman, I loved basketball. I started playing in middle school and played through four years of college. After college, I continued playing in men's and women's leagues. In fact, I was in the gym shooting baskets not long before I delivered my first child, and I was back coaching and playing three weeks later.

I continued to play four to five days a week until the summer after my twenty-seventh birthday, when I became aware my sister-in-law was struggling with a variety of addictions and offered to take in her daughter until she got herself together. Because my niece had experienced incredible trauma and needed intense support, I knew I could not be away from her or my other children during this season of life, so I promised God I would take time off from basketball. After six months, my sister-in-law got her life together and came for her daughter. A week later, I received a call initiating a chain of amazing opportunities.

Is this Erin Jones? This is the Seattle Storm.

Excuse me?

We are having an open tryout. We hear you're a baller, and we'd like to invite you to try out.

While my head was screaming, "Are you aware I'm twenty-eight years old, have small children I'm caring for, and haven't seen the inside of a gym in six months?" what spilled out of my mouth instead was, "When is the tryout?" It turned out I had three months to go from "zero" to professional, so I began to train myself at the YMCA six days a week, six hours a day. I had no idea what I was doing, but I was determined to give it my best effort.

A couple of months later, the managers of the YMCA were so impressed with my work ethic that they reached out to a professional manager and asked if he would consider supporting me for free. They knew my husband was a youth pastor, so we had little money, and we were raising small children and caring for an ailing mother. They knew I could not afford to pay for the kind of preparation required for a professional tryout. The manager, who was supporting two other players trying out for the Storm, agreed to take me on as well and informed me we would be doing physical training with an Olympic trainer.

I was so excited to join a group of women bound for a WNBA tryout! Who gets this opportunity—and at age twenty-eight?! I had played basketball at a Division III college, where I had led my team for four years, but we never had a weight room or a staff trainer. I had done all my training on my own, so the idea of having an Olympic trainer was unimaginable.

On our first day of training, my manager drove all three of us to the gym. As I pulled my sweats down over my shorts, the trainer said, "Excuse me. You are old and out of shape. There's no way I'm training you. You need to leave my gym." He was looking right at me, but I was so shocked, I couldn't believe he could be talking to me.

He continued his criticism, telling me again I was old and weak and needed to leave the gym. He was adamant he didn't have time to get me into shape and refused to associate his name with my training. When I stared blankly at him, he said more forcefully, "Did you not hear me? Leave my gym now!"

I picked up my sweats and walked out, not remembering until the door closed behind me that we had all come in one car. I had no way to get home. I stood outside the facility in tears; I felt so humiliated. But then I had a revelation. *This guy didn't get to tell me what I could or could not do. Maybe he wouldn't train me, but I could continue to train myself.*

I put my bag and sweats down on the sidewalk and began running line drills in the parking lot. An hour later, when the other ladies came out from their training, I was still running lines, and they were in disbelief I'd been running the entire time.

> **This guy didn't get to tell me what I could or could not do. Maybe he wouldn't train me, but I could continue to train myself.**

Just over a month later, I actually tried out for *two* WNBA teams: a six-hour tryout with the Seattle Storm, followed by a four-hour drive to Portland for another six-hour tryout with the Portland Fire the next day. Around lunchtime on the second day, I realized, as much as I loved basketball, I didn't love it enough to make it a profession. However, I had promised myself to show my best self, so I pushed until the last buzzer.

At the end of our tryout in Portland, a woman who had played on the very first U.S. Olympic basketball team approached me and told me she had been watching me all day and was impressed. She had noticed my leadership skills immediately and could tell by the way I carried myself that I would be a great captain for an American team she was taking to Mexico in the summer.

My summer in Mexico City was one of the greatest athletic experiences of my life. We played against several semi-professional teams and played a series of exhibition games against the Mexican national team. Between games we got to see the sights and interact with locals.

Because I had majored in Spanish and was the only American who spoke Spanish, I was able to do some translating for the team and had a huge advantage as I played with children on the streets and joined men's pick-up soccer games in community parks. People were fascinated by *la giganta* who could speak Spanish.

Within days of returning to the United States, I received a call from my cousin on my father's side who had heard about my experiences in Mexico.

Hey! I am coaching a girls' basketball camp right before school starts. Would you consider coaching with me? My girls absolutely need to meet you and hear your story.

Because my cousin lived in the same small town in Minnesota where my mother's stepmother lived—someone I had rarely had any contact with—I saw another opportunity unfold.

You see, I am adopted. Not only am I adopted, but I am a black woman who was adopted as a small child in 1971 by white parents in Minnesota. Although most of my family members were supportive and embracing, the community often was not. In fact, my parents moved to The Netherlands where they would serve as educators at the American School of The Hague for three decades. While we were overseas, my mother's mother passed away and, just weeks later, her father called to inform her he planned to remarry. We did not return to the United States for the wedding, but we did return for Christmas.

We had an incredible visit with our sixteen "new" cousins until it was time to pass out Christmas presents. Of the eighteen grandchildren, my brother and I were the only two who were not given gifts. My parents whisked us out of the house before the end of Christmas celebrations, and we spent the rest of our winter holiday with my father's family. We never spoke about this incident or visited my mother's parents again.

Although we never talked about the incident, I thought about my grandparents often and desperately wanted to understand what had happened. As I got older, I began to put pieces together, but since we didn't talk about controversial issues in my family, I knew better than to bring up my concerns. And yet, the curiosity lingered.

If I come, could you arrange for me to meet my maternal grandmother?

My cousin said, "Of course!" and I flew to Minnesota several weeks later. After the first day of camp, my cousin dropped me off at a retirement home where my grandmother, with her four-foot-eleven-inch frame, opened the door and invited me in. When she offered me some tea, I was thankful to have a few minutes to collect myself and figure out what to say to a woman I hadn't spoken to in almost twenty years.

When Grandma returned to the living room several minutes later, she was not holding tea cups. She had a shoebox in her hands, and her face was stained with tears. She put the shoe box on the table in front of me and began to take out the contents. Inside the box was every school picture ever taken of me, every certificate I had ever won, and every newspaper clipping about me. Despite what had happened between us and her many years ago, my mother had continued to send her memorabilia.

"Erin, do you know out of eighteen grandchildren, we are most proud of you?"

I was in absolute shock!

"I am so sorry your grandfather and I never told you. We just didn't know how to tell you because you were a nigger." (Yep. She said "the" word.)

"Grandma, you can't use that word."

"Well, what am I supposed to call you?"

"How about Erin?"

I realized in that moment—that opportunity created by a string of other opportunities—there was a huge difference between ignorance and racism. My grandmother had missed twenty years of my life believing she didn't know how to talk with me because she assumed we were so different.

"Erin, I know your grandfather died before he could tell you, but he loved you so much. Can you ever forgive us?"

"Grandma, I did not come all the way out here to coach a basketball camp. I came here hoping to forgive you."

We cried together for what seemed like an eternity, and I completely forgave my grandmother. She passed away within the next six months.

Some may think trying out for the WNBA at the age of twenty-eight while caring for two small children and an aging mother was a silly idea. However, had I not said *yes* to trying out for the WNBA, I would not have had the opportunity to travel to Mexico City to play against the Olympic Team. Had I not gone to Mexico, my cousin would not have thought to ask me to come to Minnesota. And had I not gone to Minnesota, I would not have had the opportunity to make peace with my grandmother before she died.

> Every opportunity—whether a girl wins or loses, succeeds or fails—will lead to her next opportunity.

Girls need to be given opportunities. And they need to be taught to recognize them and say *yes* to them. Every opportunity—whether a girl wins or loses, succeeds or fails—will lead to her next opportunity. As educators and adult leaders, make it your priority to equip your girls to recognize and embrace *all* their opportunities.

A CALL TO ACTION

★ What specific actions can you take to encourage girls to recognize and embrace opportunities?

★ Initiate a conversation with a girl about women in sports and their impact on the world.

★ If you could go back to a situation you've been in and change your approach to give yourself a better opportunity to move ahead, what would you do?

THE POWER OF ATTITUDE

CHAPTER 9

One Size Does Not Fit All

SOMETIMES I (LYNMARA) LOVE one-size-fits-all. If I'm buying a shirt or cap for someone whose size I don't know, it makes shopping easy! But when it comes to girls—especially what defines girls—one-size-fits-all rarely *fits* at all.

I must confess I love long hair. As a child I desired to be Rapunzel, but my mom kept my hair short most of the time. You can imagine my disappointment and lack of understanding when one of my daughters decided to keep her hair short. Because long hair on girls is often associated with femininity, I was worried about my daughter losing hers. I had to learn that having a confident girl who is happy and comfortable in her own skin matters more than the length of her hair. I would be lying if I said I didn't try to convince her to let it grow, but what really needed to grow was my perception of what hair symbolizes.

Another one-size-fits-all stereotype is that girls who play sports—especially those played predominantly by boys—are tomboys. I worry girls might shy away from playing predominantly male sports because of the social stigmas attached to some of those sports. Girls might be afraid of being perceived as too strong or rough. But who says femininity and beauty can't be found in a strong, determined, and fearless girl? Breaking the mold and engaging in risk-taking activities might be exactly what's needed to change the stereotypes of what girls should and shouldn't be doing.

> **But who says femininity and beauty can't be found in a strong, determined, and fearless girl?**

But are these opportunities available to girls? Research reveals "girls have 1.3 million fewer opportunities to play high school sports than boys have." Considering how much confidence, teamwork, and leadership is learned through participation in sports, in and out of schools, limiting these opportunities for girls potentially sets them at a disadvantage. I wonder what schools and communities are doing to change this situation and ensure equal access for all students.

While driving my daughters to their high school one day, I asked them about sports teams and was excited to learn a group of girls recently went to the administration and football coach to advocate for a female football team. They did not wait for the right moment. They did not wait for the right conditions. They took the matter into their own hands, disrupted conditions, and became founders of the school's first female football team. Because of them, future students will have the opportunity to play a sport predominantly played by boys.

Carol Dweck has done extensive work on mindset. I often wonder if our mindset about what girls can do is fixed. For example, stores continue to carry "girl power" shirts, sending a message that we must convince the world about how powerful girls can be. And many doll manufacturers maintain their story line of girls being responsible solely for cooking and child care.

One size does *not* fit all. Our culture has spent years associating colors, styles, and behaviors with either girls or boys. The most important thing is that our children be taught to be kind to one another and be good citizens. The length of their hair, sports they play, or colors they prefer really do not matter as long as their hearts are in the right place.

A CALL TO ACTION

★ Examine your current beliefs about what it means to be feminine. List any characteristics based on stereotypes and consider how to change your perspective. Expose girls to a variety of activities without defining criteria.

★ Encourage girls and volunteer to support them to play sports predominantly played by boys.

CHAPTER 10

Accept Crying as a Strength

I (LYNMARA) ADMIT IT: I cry sometimes. But I'm okay with it. I believe crying is a sign of strength and lets people see my human side. But I didn't always feel this way. I grew up thinking crying was a weakness. If I wanted to be perceived as a strong girl, tears had better not come out of my eyes.

I was reminded of this idea not long ago when I had a conversation with someone who believes crying is not appropriate in the workplace. As a leader who now believes in the power of vulnerability, I was shocked by that person's strong feelings about this. While I agree we are all professionals, we also carry with us amazing and powerful stories shaping us into who we are. These stories can bring with them strong emotion, and we should feel comfortable expressing it. However, even though I feel this way, I sometimes still hear the voice telling me not to let my tears come.

This was the case recently when I had a brief moment thinking about my father who passed away. I was fighting tears, scared someone would step into my office and judge me as weak or unprofessional. One of my colleagues did come in but simply asked how I was doing. When I responded, "I miss my father," tears started flowing. But instead of passing judgment, my colleague handed me a tissue and said, "It's perfectly fine to grieve. Take your time to be sad." After this I gave myself permission to be me and be honest about my feelings. I resolved to practice self-awareness about when I need to work on some emotions and even take a walk if I need to.

Unfortunately, many girls are still made to believe that if they are honest about their feelings and those feelings result in some type of emotion, then they will be seen as weak. Girls are hurt when they are shamed for crying and expressing an emotion natural to all human beings. Strong leaders are known for their social emotional IQ. In fact, their empathy, ability to emotionally connect, and vulnerability are often what make others follow them. Knowing this, why would you allow emotion to be viewed as a sign of weakness? Do not allow this stigma to make you forget you are human. Crying is often the result of words from the heart the lips can't speak.

A CALL TO ACTION

★ In what ways does vulnerability demonstrate strength?

★ How can you encourage vulnerability in the girls you associate with?

CHAPTER 11

Beauty Is as Beauty Does

From Katie Hurt, MD

I GREW UP IN A "girl world." I have two sisters, and my friends were girls who had only sisters (or brothers who were so much older or younger we didn't interact with them). I went to an all-girl Catholic high school and lived in a sorority at the University of California, Berkeley. And I grew up in the welcoming, liberal city of San Francisco, which also contributed to the "girl world" experience of my youth.

My sisters, friends, and I all became doctors, orthodontists, teachers, lawyers, wildlife biologists, accountants—whatever positions fulfilled our dreams. While our "girl world" certainly contributed to this, the biggest factor in our choices was the unending support from our parents to reach and achieve what we wanted, not what they wanted or what traditional society dictated. While nearly all of us had moms who stayed at home while our fathers worked, every one of our parents supported our interests and never doubted we could—or should—do what we wanted with our lives, even if it was outside the box of their reality.

One of my mom's favorite sayings was, "Beauty is as beauty does," meaning the *doing* of life matters, *not* how one looks. My sisters and I were always healthy, neat, and clean, but my parents never emphasized beauty, weight, style, etc. While they complimented us when we dressed up for a dance, beauty was not stressed on a daily basis. We were also shielded from the pressure to be "beautiful" by wearing a school uniform for twelve years. My parents knew the importance of being engaged in friendships and in school and community in whatever way we enjoyed, whether that was through music, student council, sports, or after-school jobs. Thanks to our parents, we were never distracted by society's definition of beauty and were encouraged to pursue our dreams.

> **"Beauty is as beauty does," meaning the *doing* of life matters, *not* how one looks.**

From an early age, my younger sister, Mollie, was deeply passionate about the outdoors and animals, despite growing up in the middle of San Francisco with parents who had no interest in camping or pets (other than a cat). When she got to high school, she joined the Student Conservation Association and spent the summer in the wilds of Zion National Park, working with trail crews and exploring her passion for conservation and wildlife.

When I was in high school, I found a summer internship shadowing a pediatric oncologist, Dr. Arthur Ablin, at the University of California San Francisco. I was not deterred by the fact no one in our family was a doctor or nurse; science was my deep-seated interest, and this was an opportunity to explore it. Not only did I observe what the pediatric oncologist did, but I got to see what the nurses, social workers, physical therapists, and radiology techs did as well.

As a biochemistry major at UC Berkeley, I wrote letters to all the professors in the biochemistry department, trying to get a position in their lab for the summer. I followed up by going to the labs personally to meet with them about a position. Giovanna Ames, PhD, one of the few women in the department, offered me a position on the spot, and I worked under an outstanding and patient postdoc, Carol Mimura, PhD, in the lab. My gender was never mentioned in relation to my abilities; it was a non-issue. Again, my "girl world" had helped me explore my interest in being a biochemist. Later, when I decided the bench wasn't for me and I wanted to pursue a career in medicine, these professors fully supported my decision and helped me with my new path and all that lay ahead.

While studying at UCSF School of Medicine, I felt I learned as much about other cultures, religions, sexuality, and gender issues as I did about the science of medicine. The AIDS epidemic had started, and UCSF and San Francisco General Hospital took pride in treating people of all backgrounds with the same dignity. As a result, I received a glorious education, making me not only a "book smart" physician but also a better physician clinically.

When I started my emergency medicine residency at UC San Diego, I received my first jolt out of my "girl world." While I had inklings of a "boy world" along the residency interview trail, when my residency director announced during orientation that our journal club would meet at Hooters, I practically fell off my chair, uttering in complete shock, "Hooters!?" Hooters represented to me all I had been protected from over the years: women being viewed as objects, an emphasis on appearance over intelligence, and stereotypes of what women could aspire to become. Having been raised as I had, and based on my experiences in college and medical school, I knew the program could educate their residents in a more balanced environment. I also had the strength and resolve to influence change. Thankfully, change did come, though not overnight as I would have preferred.

Fast forward twenty years since finishing residency. My sisters and I have learned a lot about the "boy world"—we have seven kids among us, six of whom are boys! While I've received a great and humbling education parenting two boys, my goal is still to raise them as I was raised, but with this twist: "Handsome is as handsome does."

A CALL TO ACTION

★ Pay attention to the content of your compliments to girls and women. Are they related to beauty or intellect?

★ Talk about girls' bodies in regard to the great things they are capable of doing rather than their appearance.

CHAPTER 12

Change the Rules

I (**Lynmara**) **like to know** the rules to everything. They provide me with structure and a roadmap. However, I have learned some rules do not apply to certain scenarios, even when the game looks the same. Let me explain.

I grew up in a very conservative household in a culture where women take care of the family while men go to work. Those were the rules. While I knew many women who also worked outside the home, every decision about their education and career revolved around this question: "How will it impact my ability to do everything I need to do as a mom and wife?" As long as those things weren't compromised, women could chase their dreams. Unfortunately, I have seen many friends back home compromise their dreams because they kept them from perfectly fulfilling their traditional roles. And they had to be okay with this because another rule we grew up with was that women had to pretend they were perfectly happy with the rules. In this environment, if they wanted to do more, they waited until everyone else in the family had fulfilled their dreams, and then they could chase their own.

When I first came to the United States in 1999 from Puerto Rico, I, like many women from my country, had gotten used to playing by the rules and putting myself last, thinking only men could provide for and contribute to a family. Moving to the United States, however, gave me a different perspective and showed me I could have a great education, career, and raise a family as well. I met amazing women doing *all* of these. As I asked them about balance and how they managed to check all the boxes, I learned they adjusted the rules a bit. Some let go of a perfectly clean house, while others moved away from preparing three-course meals every night, but all of them ensured they stayed true to themselves along the way.

> **As you raise strong girls, pay attention to the message you are sending about what is acceptable and what is not.**

As you raise strong girls, pay attention to the message you are sending about what is acceptable and what is not. My hope is we come together to build up a generation of women unafraid to speak up and demonstrate a better way to pursue dreams. This is one of the reasons I will always be open about making Crockpot meals, taking cleaning shortcuts, and saying *no* to what might have been expected in order to allow me to do things supporting my dream. Living this way has given me clarity and freedom to pursue dreams I never thought I could go after. This does not mean I am not willing to compromise. But I want my girls—and all girls—to know it is totally acceptable to make room for what makes them better people, women, and leaders. I want this generation to understand that success comes with hard work, and reaching it sometimes means the rules of the game need to be changed.

A CALL TO ACTION

★ Write down your definition of balance.

★ Encourage girls to focus on self-care (exercise, healthy diet, adequate sleep).

★ Teach girls the value of establishing priorities (family, friends, school).

CHAPTER 13

Inspire Greatness through Challenge

From Erin Jones, educator and speaker

I **TRY TO RUN THREE** miles a day at least five days a week. I don't run because I love running. I *love* playing basketball, but I'm almost fifty and in a season of my life when playing basketball doesn't make sense. It's difficult to find regular games with the crazy schedule I keep, and my body doesn't recover quickly from the jarring and injuries I get from landing funny or diving for a loose ball, so running makes much more sense for staying in shape.

I began running after I lost an election for state superintendent of public education by less than one percent—and as the first black woman in my state to run for statewide office. My best friend suggested I prepare to run a half-marathon. While I wasn't excited about the idea, she suggested I set a goal I could completely control after my election loss. I would be in charge of my training, and I would determine whether or not I completed the race.

I started in December running one mile a day five days a week. I pushed up to two miles a day in January, and by the end of March, I was running three miles a day. By May I was running three miles *three times* a day and five to seven miles two days a week. In June of 2017, I ran my first half-marathon—thirteen plus miles with no stop, not even for water. I even sprinted the last one hundred yards.

> **If I can make it to mile three, I can run for miles, and I feel like I can accomplish anything.**

What a sense of accomplishment!

Since then, I have committed to continue my running regimen. I try to run half-marathons, 5Ks, and 10Ks once a quarter to give myself something to shoot for. I also run five to six times a week. I practice pushing through discomfort to get used to the realities of challenge and to practice not giving up. Every time I run, during the first mile I wonder why I am running. In the second mile, my body hurts, and I want to quit. But if I can make it to mile three, I can run for miles, and I feel like I can accomplish anything.

Running has taught me the importance of setting goals and that every great accomplishment comes in response to challenge and discomfort. I have learned greatness is not born in the *absence* of challenge but in *response* to it.

As an educator and leader, you have an opportunity and responsibility to teach this lesson to the girls you work with. Challenge them to set a goal just beyond their reach, something that's realistic but requires them to stretch their current abilities, skills, or beliefs about themselves. Encourage them to practice every day and push through the challenge and discomfort and assure them greatness lies in their response to the pain and their pursuit of the goal.

A CALL TO ACTION

★ Share with a girl what you have learned through personal challenge and discomfort.

★ Set a personal goal, realistic but just beyond your reach, and create a specific plan for achieving it.

CHAPTER 14

Point beyond Physical Beauty

GIRLS FACE A LOT of pressure: to be domestic, build a career, live a fairy-tale life, etc. On top of these expectations, they are also constantly pressured to be perfect and beautiful. Magazines send messages of flawless skin, perfect bodies, and popularity. Girls worry about their weight and physical appearance while media continue to send messages about what the world defines as beauty, making it difficult for girls to build strong self-esteem. Without a solid foundation, girls might believe this type of beauty is a requirement to be successful and that the approval of others is the only thing that matters.

Because the consequences of this mindset can be damaging, teaching girls about beauty beyond the exterior is critical. Teach and equip girls to fight these negative messages and empower them to focus on their internal beauty. Share conversations with young girls early about how these messages can be destructive to their development. Team up and change how beauty is defined by sending the message that beauty is about attitude and heart.

The reality is that attractiveness is subjective. Everyone sees beauty in different places and in different ways. Meghan Markle loves her freckles and embraces them, while others might see them as imperfections needing to be concealed and covered. Ultimately these differences in our exteriors make our world a beautiful collage of diverse colors and shapes.

Send a strong message: Beauty is more than physical appearance. Beauty is also found in personality, confidence, intelligence, compassion, friendship, and sharing space with others.

> Send a strong message: Beauty is more than physical appearance.

So what is beauty beyond a selfie? What does it mean to be beautiful beyond filters? I (Lynmara) am afraid many have forgotten that body and face do not make a girl beautiful. Create spaces where the light of the soul is the place where true beauty is found, and your girls have the chance to feel loved, strong, and pure beyond their physical appearance.

A CALL TO ACTION

★ Share positive affirmations with girls, highlighting aspects besides beauty.
★ Expose girls to media that focuses on health and growth, instead of physical beauty.

CHAPTER 15

Urge Them to Control Their Narrative

From Sanée Bell, principal

WHEN I WAS IN my twenties, I read *Letters to My Younger Self*, a compilation of stories written by famous women sharing wisdom gained from their life experiences. The women were all different ages, so I could immediately relate to some of the stories, while others served as advice about the future—potential pitfalls, joy and sadness, and hope that everything would turn out all right. I especially enjoyed this book because it provided me with free advice without anyone knowing I was struggling. Plus, it was free of judgment. Now, in my forties, I wish I could have told myself then that everything *was* going to turn out all right.

When I was twelve, my parents divorced, and my family's world turned upside down. We struggled for money, which meant at a time when appearance was so important to me, I had very little. My mother couldn't afford the latest fashions and trends, so I wasn't able to look and dress the certain way I wanted. And I couldn't understand why others were able to have so much when we had so little.

Looking back, I realize I made several decisions during this time that ultimately shaped my future experiences and the woman I've become. Instead of dwelling on what I didn't have, I focused on what I could do well. I was able to meet people easily, and this gave me the opportunity to connect with others who made me a better person. I learned very quickly I did not like middle school "drama" because it bred negativity, which squelched positive energy and opportunities to do anything good. I learned drama only has power if it has participants, so in situations where others were "stirring the pot," I removed myself or remained quiet if there was no way to escape. Staying out of drama as a teen helped me become a positive adult who is able to get along well with others.

I also played sports through middle school and high school, which helped me build self-confidence. While I wasn't the best player on the team, I always did *my* best. I believed my contribution to the team was valuable, and no one could play my role better. I learned I had to be my own first fan; if I don't believe I'm great, why should someone else? I worked to put myself in positions where I could achieve my personal best.

I also tried not to compare myself to others because when I did, I always found a way to be the loser. However, when I learned to like myself for what I had to offer, I began to love myself. And once I loved myself, I did whatever I needed to do to make myself better. And since the temptation to compare myself to others didn't go away when I became an adult, I'm glad I learned at an early age how to compare myself only with me. It has helped me stay focused on making sure I'm the best possible *me* I can be. Comparison is the thief of joy, and I don't want anyone or anything to steal my joy.

Playing sports also helped me stay focused on my academics. I knew the only way to a better life—which I thought at the time meant having more "things"—was to get an education. I became the first person in my immediate and extended family to graduate from college. I was fortunate to have so many teachers who believed in me and made a difference for me. I connected with the teachers who really enjoyed what they did and genuinely cared for me, giving me a strong safety net and a sense of courage and confidence to fight through challenges.

During my first year of teaching, I tried to mentor several students whom I saw greatness in, though they didn't see it in themselves. I connected immediately with one young lady who had Vitiligo, a condition causing the loss of skin color. She was one of my favorite students because of her bubbly personality, but I didn't know she was hurting inside. She spent every free moment in my classroom and found ways to be in my presence. I thought she just liked my class because I was an awesome teacher!

> When I learned to like myself for what I had to offer, I began to love myself. And once I loved myself, I did whatever I needed to do to make myself better.

After she became an adult, I learned she had liked being around me because I helped her discover herself and what she was worth, and I had given her hope. When I asked her what she had struggled with as a teen and why she had connected with me so well, she said, "I struggled with self-esteem and identity. You gave me confidence. You told me to respect my body. You were more than a teacher. You were a role model. I learned to love myself because of you. I felt worthy. I stopped wearing makeup [to even out my skin color] after you told me I was beautiful."

Needless to say, I was touched by her words. She is now a successful motivational speaker who shares her story to inspire other young women.

Looking back, I realize if I hadn't made the decisions I made at an early age—if I hadn't written my own narrative to focus on what I could do well, be positive, and get an education—my story may have never included this precious student. And her story may have been very different as well. My own "letter to my younger self" would assure her everyone has a story. Characters and situations may enter without permission, but she is the author of her own story, and she has the power to write out unwanted characters and change the scene. She controls the narrative. She can define who she is and what she can accomplish in life.

A CALL TO ACTION

★ Write a letter to your future self, including your dreams and fears. Be specific about your plan to make your mark on the world. Put your letter where you can look at it periodically to see how you are progressing toward becoming your future self.

★ What have you done to create your own narrative? How can you empower girls to create their *best* narrative?

CHAPTER 16

Yes, Girls Can!

TOO MANY GIRLS HAVE grown up believing their potential roles are limited. We were propelled to write this book because we believe girls should have *unlimited* roles and opportunities! And we are urging *you*—those who work with girls in schools, homes, and communities—to join us in saying, *Yes! Girls **can***:

- run for class president—or President of the United States!
- snow ski black diamond runs
- play kickball with the boys
- dress up any way they want for Halloween
- write code and program computers
- start their own businesses as an entrepreneur
- make important decisions

- lead movements and change
- play any sport they choose
- become influencers—inventors—disruptors
- change the status quo
- have a voice—and be heard
- fulfill their dreams

A CALL TO ACTION

★ What traditionally "male-only" things have you seen girls do or encouraged girls to do?

★ What steps can you take to change the narrative for girls around you?

CHAPTER 17

Girls Are Not "Guys"

From Kim Darche, instructional coach

DOES USING THE TERM "guys" to refer to a room of boys and girls communicate girls are not as important to recognize? Even writing those words hurts. However, calling a group of males and females "guys" has long been an accepted practice. In fact, it has become commonplace to the point that most people are unaware of how often they use it when speaking to mixed company until someone points it out to them. (Tomorrow you will be painfully aware of how often you use it.)

What would happen if you referred to a classroom of boys and girls or a staff meeting with men and women as *girls* or *ladies*? How would the men in the room react? Can you imagine trying this in a middle school classroom? My guess is you'll get a reaction similar to the one I received a few years ago.

One of my students at a scholastic competition was a boy with longer hair who was on a team with three female students. At the conclusion of a round, they were collectively called "girls." Hot diggity, if all those students weren't outraged, asking me how this could happen. I just smiled and politically correctly answered, "I am sure it was just a mistake." But I guarantee, at one point during the following week, those same students were in a class at school where the teacher said, "All right, guys, listen up," and they did not respond in an uproar.

> **What would happen if you referred to a classroom of boys and girls, or a staff meeting with men and women, as *girls* or *ladies*?**

Perhaps I have become overly sensitive. Maybe I am turning into the proverbial lady, yelling at kids to get off her lawn. But I do know the term "guys" is being routinely used as gender neutral in classrooms, in PLCs, and in educators' professional development.

If you had a class made up of Dannys and Lilys and called out, "Okay Dannys, attention over here for a moment," who would look up? Just the Dannys, right? And you would expect *only* the Dannys to give their attention. However, saying "Ok, guys!" is considered perfectly acceptable, and you expect everyone in the room to respond to it. I attended an all-girl Catholic high school with only five male teachers. Even there the term *guys* was used when, actually, all the "guys" were across the parking lot at the all-boys school!

I am grateful I attended an all-girl high school where girls held the leadership positions. We were the leads in the plays and the star athletes (Not me, but others definitely were!). We were empowered by our female environment. While single-gender schools are uncommon today, educators can strive to empower females within the educational system by making one small change: saying "guys and gals" instead of just "guys." Many teachers are already doing this. I observed a teacher who referred to her students this way when she wanted to draw them back and focus on the lesson. She never missed a beat, and she never slipped and called the class "guys."

She is making the change.

I can already hear some of you saying, "It is not such a big deal!" Maybe it is not a big deal for you, but to the girls you teach and the women with whom you work, it is a *very big deal* and can make a lasting impact.

So why not join the teacher above and try some of these: *All right,* _____, *listen up*!

- guys and gals (or really mix it up with gals and guys!)
- team
- y'all
- folks
- everyone
- colleagues
- fellow coffee drinkers
- learners
- writers
- students
- friends
- people
- users of the seventh-grade copier

Be creative. Be inclusive. Empower girls in a seemingly insignificant—but actually, oh, so significant—way!

A CALL TO ACTION

★ Before you address a group, think about what you are going to call them and be sure to address them with an inclusive term.

★ How can you spread an inclusive message when talking to a diverse group of students?

"It is to our own detriment that we underestimate the might of small and simple things."

—Richelle E. Goodrich

CHAPTER 18

Courage Is a Superpower

"The defense of our nation is a shared responsibility. Women have served in the defense of this land for years before our United States was born. They have contributed their talents, skills, and courage to this endeavor for more than two centuries with an astounding record of achievement that stretches from Lexington and Concord to the Persian Gulf and beyond."

**—Retired General Gordon R. Sullivan
Chief of Staff of the Army, 1991–1995**

GIRLS ARE STRONG AND courageous, and they should be allowed—even encouraged—to demonstrate their courage in any way they choose. Coming to the United States from another country without speaking the language and stepping into uncomfortable situations required strength, but I (Lynmara) never considered myself courageous. However, as a school leader, I learned courage was required in many situations where I faced extraordinary challenges. Many obstacles required me to step out of my comfort zone to make decisions and have conversations many may have found unpopular.

All girls will face similar obstacles at some point, which raises a number of questions in my mind:

- When will they learn the skills needed to overcome these obstacles?
- Are girls being allowed to wrestle with issues, putting them in a place where courage is required?
- Are they encouraged to speak up for what they strongly believe is right?
- How do young girls learn about boundaries and how to hold others accountable for their actions?

I recently heard a high school senior share during a speech that she intended to apply to the Naval Academy. Some at my table whispered, "I am sure she will not be planning to have a family," and, "It must be so hard." As someone who deeply cares for our soldiers, I found these comments surprising and heartbreaking, and I responded to them by saying, "If my daughters wanted to serve, I would be filled with joy and pride. Nothing is more courageous than choosing to serve one's country." Some of the people corrected themselves, saying they did not mean it in a stereotypical way.

Data from the Pentagon reported by CNN notes that in 2011, more than 200,000 women were in the active-duty military, including sixty-nine generals and admirals. This means women made up only approximately fifteen percent of the 1.4 million active-duty soldiers. The number of women actually holding jobs that put them in the battlefield was even less.

Lisa Meyers, an officer in the United States Army, remembers her recruitment vividly. Her male recruiter kept offering her clerical and medical jobs. However, convicted by her purpose for wanting to serve, she kept pushing for jobs to put her in combat zones. Lisa said the recruiter was persistent and kept telling her she would have an "easier" transition if she took a non-combat job, but Lisa felt confident about her athletic background and didn't want to consider anything besides a combat job. Not until after her entrance scores came back did he consider her athletic history and better understand her desire to serve in infantry. When she arrived at the Advanced Individual Training school, she better understood the recruiter's concerns. There were only three females in Lisa's group of thirty. However, despite this, Lisa formed a tight bond with her fellow female soldiers, and they often shared with one another what they would do if they had the opportunity to become high-ranking officers.

> **Women can be confident and courageous *while* being feminine and showing emotions.**

Since then Lisa has had the opportunity to go to many academies and schools, allowing her to advance in her military career. She has done several tours to war zones, and while she finds it hard to be away from home, she still feels as passionately as she did the day she enlisted and wishes more girls would join the Service. She thinks people expect females in the military to look or behave differently than what is traditionally seen as feminine. But she believes, as I do, women can be confident and courageous *while* being feminine and showing emotions. Lisa summed up this idea well when she said, "Yes, I have been trained to be strong and to stay focused, but . . . at the end of the day, when I pull out my bun and let my hair loose, I am a woman with a heart. Courage is more than fighting."

A CALL TO ACTION

- ★ Normalize setbacks. Assure girls that some failures make them more courageous. Prepare them to deal with unplanned situations.
- ★ Create a space where failure is allowed. Show self-compassion.
- ★ How can you encourage girls to be courageous in their routine activities?
- ★ How can you encourage girls to be courageous by stepping into roles predominantly filled by boys?

CHAPTER 19

Knock Down Roadblocks

From Thomas C. Murray, director of innovation

I N EARLY 2010, I became a father for the first time. Paisley Addison entered my world, forever making it a better place. As parents and educators, my wife and I immediately had vast hopes for Paisley's future. We wanted to provide every opportunity for our little angel to follow her dreams and do anything in life she wanted. If you're a parent, you can relate. You want nothing to stand in the way of your child having every possible opportunity. Unfortunately, challenged by today's societal norms, Paisley will likely face greater challenges than her brother, born three years later. This is why I do the work I do. Simply put, I want my little girl—and *all* girls—to be able to follow their hopes and dreams, running through roadblocks if necessary, and do what they want to do in this life

At the age of eight, Paisley loves technology and she loves to code. Her device is one of her favorite possessions, and she uses it actively and passively. Sometimes she wants to consume the latest movie or TV show; other times she chooses to design, code, and create—perhaps a city in Minecraft, a house using a professional home design app, or an obstacle course for one of her robots. However, for girls like Paisley, whose passions may fall into an area society has traditionally deemed more appropriate for boys, opportunities to pursue these passions haven't always been available, and the opportunities are even fewer for females of color.

To see the context of these disparities and how this is a massive equity issue to overcome, consider *Anatomy of an Enduring Gender Gap: The Evolution of Women's Participation in Computer Science*, a 2015 research study analyzing students' interest levels in computer science over the forty-year period from 1971 to 2011. While the study cites a wide range of student interest levels, females were continuously underrepresented. The report outlines two key findings:

- Women with artistic or social activist leanings haven't perceived computer science as complementary to their skills.
- Girls' confidence in their own math abilities is deteriorating.

So why does this gap exist? Although this issue is complex, I believe sexism remains rampant and, undoubtedly, impacts the psyche of our girls from an early age. For example, what do you see when you walk down the toy aisle in most retail stores? On one side, you find games and tools to design, create, build, or take risks. On the other side? You find an assortment of items focused on cooking and taking care of others.

Let me be clear. If these stereotypical toys are loved by the traditional gender, great! If they are embraced by the non-traditional gender, great! May *all* kids thrive in what they want to do. This conversation isn't about limiting—or pushing—one gender into particular roles. And at a macro level, it's not ultimately about empowering girls to become software engineers or computer programmers (unless *they* want to). This conversation is about providing access, opportunity, and empowerment for *all kids* to leverage their gifts and abilities to do what *they* want to do.

Paisley and girls like her, whose passions fall into an area society has traditionally deemed more appropriate for boys, are my *why*, my purpose and passion for the work I do with school districts across the nation each day. I won't stand for the inequity. If Paisley's interests and passions shine in the world of coding, my obligation is to make these opportunities available for her and countless other girls too. As a dad and an educator, I'm committed to unleashing their incredible genius—their courage, their leadership, and their brilliance. Society needs to empower girls to blow through traditionally male-dominated stereotypes and redefine these societal norms, for their future and for the *world's* future.

Fortunately, in recent years, a synergy has resulted from making STEM (Science, Technology, Engineering, and Math, or STEAM when the Arts are included) accessible to all students. Through initiatives like Hour of Code and Computer Science for All, equity in opportunity for females *and* students of color has been brought to the forefront of education. Rightfully so, as it's been desperately needed.

> **This conversation is about providing access, opportunity, and empowerment for *all kids* to leverage their gifts and abilities to do what *they* want to do.**

Changes have also started in the typical high school computer science classrooms in the United States, which have been statistically dominated by white males, while females and students of color have been despicably underrepresented. Truly, this is one of the greatest kindergarten-through-twelfth-grade equity issues. Fortunately, many schools across the country are working diligently to change this and ensure all students feel welcomed and encouraged and have equal opportunity.

I'm personally grateful for organizations like Future Ready Schools™ and Girls Who Code with missions to create equitable opportunities. Founded with the single mission of closing the gender gap in technology, Girls Who Code is working to create a dynamic pipeline of future female engineers. From after-school clubs, like those seen in the Parkland School District in Pennsylvania where Paisley is a student, to summer immersion programs, this organization is providing girls with access and opportunity to learn coding and develop the skills needed for the technology jobs that will be prevalent in the future.

As my little girl and as a female in our society who deserves equal and unlimited opportunities, Paisley is at the heart of my personal *why*. I embrace the words of comedian Michael Jr., who said, "When you know your *why*, your *what* has more impact because you are walking in or towards your purpose." I'll continue to run toward my purpose—for my own kids but also for those I'll never meet. I'll continue to work to create opportunities, not just for my own precious Paisley but for all the other girls who, just like her, may choose a device over a doll, coding instead of cooking, or leading rather than following.

A CALL TO ACTION

★ Many people say coding is the new foreign language. How can you create opportunities for the girls in your life to learn this language?

★ To get your girls excited about coding, take them to a local technology company and introduce them to the female engineers.

CHAPTER 20

Pursue the Path to Equality

WHILE EQUALITY ISSUES HAVE changed quite a bit since 1970, there is still much work to do when it comes to gender and equity, especially for women of color. Attending to this critical issue now will allow us to raise amazing girls who will be advocates of equality in the future.

I (Lynmara) am often asked, "What are you?" Initially, I was confused; I didn't understand the question. In my head I thought, "I am a human. I am the daughter of a black man and a Hispanic woman with light skin—two individuals with different skin colors who loved each other." This was my normal. However, as I navigated the world, I quickly realized this was not "normal" to others. Even my mother didn't think my curly hair was "normal," so instead of teaching me to love it, she tried every relaxer under the sun to straighten my hair like hers. While I am sure she meant well, the pain my head endured convinced me curly hair was actually beautiful. Today I embrace my natural hair and despise using any product that would change it.

When I became the robotics coach at a school where I taught, a similar thing seemed to occur. Many questioned my ability to lead the team simply because I was a female, asking, "How is she going to teach this? Isn't this for really smart people?" I ignored them and led the team for three years, focusing on recruiting minority students, specifically students with special needs. They had a blast and learned to lead while collaborating and having fun. I looked for other female coaches at every competition, but there weren't many. Thankfully, as the years have passed, I have noticed more women participating, giving me hope as we continue to advocate for girls' involvement in science and technology fields.

> Many questioned my ability to lead the team simply because I was a female, asking, "How is she going to teach this? Isn't this for really smart people?"

The work can start as early as in elementary school. Opportunities need to be created for girls of color, and educators need to be supported to intentionally recruit them. While some companies are making great advances in the fight for equality by hosting weekend "coding for girls" events to encourage them to be involved in STEM activities, these offerings cannot replace the need for educators to prioritize girls' participation in these types of extracurricular activities at school. This is the way to carve a deep path toward equality.

Depending on where they live and what school they attend, some girls might be at an advantage for participating in these activities. Unfortunately, for those living in poverty, many of whom are girls of color, we have seen teachers focus them on the academics of reading and math instead of encouraging them to enroll in extracurricular STEM opportunities. I have engaged in many conversations with educators who argue against the value of providing students with STEM opportunities when there is a greater need to get them reading at their grade level. While academics are important, I fear focusing only on this will exclude minority girls from participating in activities that promote leadership skills and can increase opportunities for scholarships. Educators have a tremendous opportunity to start or encourage more conversation about how we can support minority girls in these activities.

A CALL TO ACTION

★ Compliment a girl's participation in activities traditionally focused on boys and encourage them to participate further.

★ How can you promote equality of opportunity among the girls you work with?

★ Organize a STEM-related activity after school and recruit girls of color to participate.

CHAPTER 21

Promote the American Dream

OUR COUNTRY HAS ALWAYS promised the "American Dream"—the opportunity for all people to find or create a life better than the one they had previously, one where they can fulfill their hopes and aspirations. Unfortunately, many have to overcome great challenges, roadblocks, and even discrimination to achieve their American Dream. You have a unique opportunity—and *responsibility*—to empower girls, especially girls of color, by working to break down these roadblocks and eliminate discrimination.

As I (Lynmara) prepared to share this story, probably the most difficult chapter for me to write, my pain was still fresh, even though the event occurred two years ago. I was still crying (likely because I never fully recovered), embarrassed I had to endure such humiliation at thirty-seven years of age. While writing this chapter hopefully allowed me to grieve and heal, I trust it also allows you to understand what many people experience on a daily basis. My wish is you feel inspired to take action when you notice situations like these.

In 2016, I led a school I could refer to as a mini-United Nations, populated by students with diverse nationalities, cultures, beliefs, and values. Our staff was also extremely diverse. They understood the needs of diverse students, bringing a valuable perspective about how to engage families and meet kids where they are.

During a staff meeting to discuss our Positive Behavior Intervention Systems initiative and how we would support the students, we discussed the importance of considering this diversity, since students from various cultures respond differently to discipline, parent-teacher interactions, and incentives. I stressed the importance of being cognizant of students' cultures when determining consequences for behavior.

As a leader, I have always taken pride in giving my staff the voice to challenge others' thinking, and I value their feedback. The staff seemed responsive during the meeting and gave helpful comments. However, after the meeting, I checked the "parking lot," an area near the door where staff could leave written comments, feedback, and questions we did not cover during the meeting, and found a note I have since memorized because of its deep impact on me: "I am not sure what the big deal is about minority kids, boys and girls, and discipline. This is the United States. They should get with the program. I cannot understand why we keep talking about this. If you live in the U.S., get with the program."

My heart sank. My jaw dropped. Tears came rolling down my face. Those helping me clean up asked what had happened, but I hid the note. I could not share what I had read. In fact, I immediately went home after the meeting and called my supervisor, who was extremely supportive. I wanted to quit. I felt I had no business working with someone who felt this way. My mind was racing, "Who wrote this note? Why do they think this way?"

For days I continued to be sad. I read the note over and over, trying to understand why this person felt the need to express these feelings. My staff noticed I was sad and asked if they could help with anything. Weeks later the person who wrote the note confessed and later decided to move, explaining he or she was overwhelmed by politics and the expectation to learn how to deal with an array of cultures. I accepted the apology; it was the right thing to do, and I wanted to model the grace I had been given multiple times. But it still hurt to think about how many others are discriminated against and continue to suffer, wondering if they belong.

> I wanted to model the grace I had been given multiple times. But it still hurt to think about how many others are discriminated against and continue to suffer, wondering if they belong.

This was the first time since I moved to the United States that I had experienced such a situation. It has made me advocate harder for those discriminated against and makes me more intentional about my work and the message of "cultural awareness" when it comes to our students. Even though I still hear on a daily basis about the struggles some minority students experience, I maintain hope as people become more educated about these issues.

As a female leader, this experience made a tremendous impact on me. It changed my approach to seeing and tackling difficult issues. I learned kindness can still be shown to those who do not share my views. I also learned I could preserve people's integrity and show them love in the midst of conflict and hurt.

While I am thankful for those lessons, I suffered a big loss in my spirit as a result of this interaction. I let the event affect me in such a way I wanted to leave. But this would not have been the best choice. I am so glad I was able to come back and kindly show grace to someone different from me. I was able to put Dr. Martin Luther King's message into action and stand up for what I believed was right. Now I feel inspired to do the same and carry the message that no matter where you come from, you can live the American Dream. This is my legacy to minority students and girls—teaching them that living the American Dream is more than just arriving in America.

A CALL TO ACTION

★ How can you teach girls to be confident and assertive and stand up for equity and justice?

★ Encourage girls to express positive *and* negative feelings in a respectful manner.

★ Put girls in situations where they have to make decisions.

CHAPTER 22

Disrupt the Narrative

From Erin Jones, educator, speaker

INEVER INTENDED TO BECOME an administrator. When I began teaching, my plan was to teach until I could no longer stand. However, in 2008 I won recognition as the Milken Educator of the Year for Washington State and, as a result, was invited to apply for a position at the Office of Superintendent of Public Instruction. At the end of the school year, I began working as a Director at the State and was promoted to Assistant State Superintendent for Student Achievement one year later.

I arrived twenty minutes early for my first cabinet meeting, and as I prepared to enter the room, I heard voices inside:

"Hey! Do you know who this Erin Jones girl is?"

"Well, we've been getting a lot of crap about being a bunch of old white guys. We need a pretty, young, black girl on the cabinet to shut people up."

I froze in my tracks. How could I go into the room now? Could I *ever* go into the room? Had I only been promoted because I was just the "pretty, young, black girl" and they needed a brown face at the table?

I went quickly to the restroom, afraid the tears were going to explode from my face and people would see me as immature or weak, before I even stepped into a leadership role. About five minutes before the meeting began, I stood in front of the mirror, fixed my lipstick, added some face powder, straightened my blouse, and resolved I would not be deterred. I walked straight and tall into the meeting room, as if I were entering for the first time.

A couple of weeks later, I learned I was making at least $10,000 less than the next-lowest paid person on staff, a man who had been promoted to the cabinet at the same time I was and in a similar role. When I asked my boss about this discrepancy, he told me the lower salary represented my inexperience, since I had never served as an administrator. He told me, "You need to do your time."

But this didn't make sense. Some on the cabinet had never worked in a school building, and others had not worked as administrators. And one of the gentlemen on the cabinet who *had* been an administrator for decades was not comfortable writing agendas for meetings or confident facilitating meetings, yet I was already doing both.

> **Historically, men negotiate in this way, but women often do not . . . . They are taught to be compliant and humble.**

In retrospect, I realize that before accepting the new position, I should have done my homework to determine the salaries of others on the cabinet, and I should have negotiated for the salary I deserved instead of taking the one they gave to me. Historically, men negotiate in this way, but women often do not. They often do not speak up when they are mistreated or spoken ill of by their peers or supervisors. They are taught to be compliant and humble. They are discouraged from demonstrating confidence, as this is seen as arrogant or as an attempt to rise above their station, whereas confident men are elevated and revered.

All these narratives must be disrupted. As a state-recognized leader, I get to challenge the stereotypes preventing women from having access to the same opportunities for leadership and positions of authority men have. All educators must do the same. Girls must be given equal access to the academic process, especially in areas where preference is often given to boys.

My Gmail tag line is, *The number one job of every adult is to be a mirror to reflect the beauty and talent of every child who comes into their path.* This truly is the most important job of every educator. Educators have an obligation to ensure every girl knows she can do math and science—or any other academic subject—well. They have a responsibility to assure girls they can be leaders and be *strong*. They have an obligation to disrupt the narrative telling girls they *can't* and teach girls to rewrite their own narrative saying they *can*!

A CALL TO ACTION

★ Mentor girls on how to calculate their personal value and negotiate a salary.

★ How can you specifically empower girls to rewrite their own narratives?

THE
POWER
OF
ENCOURAGEMENT

CHAPTER 23

Raise Girls to Lead

PEOPLE OFTEN ASK, "ARE leaders born or made?" Personally, I (Lynmara) believe a leader resides within everyone. While many girls will eventually find the leader within themselves, they need not wait. With some intentional direction from their own leaders—be they parents, teachers, coaches, church leaders, etc.—girls can be raised from an early age to be strong leaders. Every girl deserves the opportunity to develop leadership skills to equip her to run a business—or the world, if she chooses to!

One way I started developing my leadership skills was through journaling. One of my middle school Spanish teachers encouraged us to write daily, and this allowed me to put into words my dreams and goals. Every time I reread my journals and saw a goal I had not yet accomplished, something stirred inside me to go after it again with even more enthusiasm and grit. I have practiced journaling since I was young, and it continues to be a practice key to my leadership as an adult.

Research shows there is great power in writing. Not only does it help one learn more, but it helps improve communication skills as well. Unfortunately, with the increase of technology and decrease in writing assignments, girls have fewer opportunities to write in school. As a result, you must be intentional about encouraging girls to journal at home.

Teaching girls public speaking skills and giving them opportunities to present publicly is another way to help raise them to be leaders. As a principal, I loved being invited to classrooms to see students present. Our teachers were purposeful about exposing students—even students as young as first graders—to public speaking. I applaud this because I was not afforded this opportunity until high school. Because I hadn't been taught public speaking, I would sweat the night before a presentation and pray the teacher was absent the next day. PowerPoint hadn't been invented yet, which meant I had to use a stack of index cards and a poster presentation, making matters even worse.

Teaching girls to communicate and speak in public is key to raising them to be leaders. Multiple studies show most people fear public speaking, yet being good at it can help young girls form strong relationships and advance in their careers. Schools can support this effort by moving away from just giving tests and encouraging students to present their findings instead. Another alternative is to ensure every unit of study affords time for collaboration among students and ends with a speech in front of the class. Outside of school, different organizations often look for girls who are willing to share their stories. Training girls to communicate *now* is essential if you are investing in the next female president of the United States!

As a principal, I was not a fan of homework, and I am not a fan as a parent either. One reason is that I believe children should have time to engage in non-school-related activities. Whether they're involved in sports, music, arts, or a club, these activities help them become leaders in other areas beside academics. My parents could not afford for me to participate in extracurricular activities, and my school did not offer any either. In desperation, I started the eco-club at my school, but I wish I would have had a mentor to help me navigate leadership at this young age.

Recently, after one of my speaking sessions, I met a teacher who had formed a club for girls who wanted to become scientists. She told me some of her colleagues were excited about her goals for the club, but they did not seem to understand her desire to inspire *girls* to pursue science careers. When flyers about the group were not distributed on time and attendance was low, she wondered if the statistics about girls not liking science were true. However, thanks to the power of social media, more girls learned about the club from what the club members were posting and wanted to participate. As I listened to her story, I wondered what would have happened if she had stopped her efforts. Clearly, this group of girls—whom she described as "rocking the lab coats!"—would have missed an amazing opportunity.

> ## Training girls to communicate *now* is essential if you are investing in the next female president of the United States!

When was the last time you asked a girl about her passion? If recently, kudos to you! If it's been a while, do not worry—you are not alone. Most adults only talk about passion when referring to their hobbies or fulfilling careers. However, people who know their passion from an early age have a better chance of being successful and leading in life. You have likely heard of genius kids who go to college at age ten. Reports reveal one common trait these children share is knowing their passion. Can you imagine a young girl mixing crayons to make lipstick who suddenly discovers she wants to be a chemist? Or a girl who gathers friends to play soccer during recess and discovers at her young age she wants to coach a sports team?

Those who teach and coach and lead girls can raise them up to be leaders by giving them opportunities to develop leadership skills and by always highlighting their strengths in an effort to empower and guide them to find their passion. Engage girls in discovering what they are good at and help them become aware of their cognitive, social, and emotional strengths. Join others in raising female leaders!

A CALL TO ACTION

★ Intentionally give girls opportunities to lead in a variety of settings.

★ Encourage girls to participate in national organizations.

★ Share your personal dreams and successes with girls.

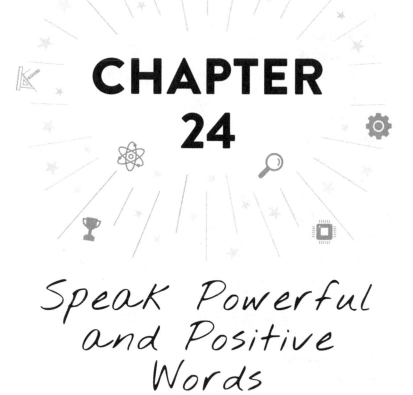

CHAPTER 24

Speak Powerful and Positive Words

WHEN YOU TALK TO girls, are you using encouraging and positive language? What girls hear repeatedly from others in their lives makes a tremendous impact on them. Your language is one of the greatest tools you have to influence girls, so ensure your words are powerful and positive. In your daily speech with girls, incorporate phrases like:

I believe in you.

I know you can.

You can do whatever you want to do and be whoever you want to be.

You deserve a seat at the table.

Those girls are doing it; you can too.

You matter.

Way to lead!

You were born to do this.

You can rule the world.

You can influence others.

Go after it.

Don't stop.

You can be a great force.

Go be amazing.

You are strong.

You can change the world.

We need girls like you.

You are an inspiration.

Keep trying.

You are fearless.

You are graceful.

You do not have to depend on someone else to tell you who you are.

Do not be afraid of mistakes.

Follow your heart.

Be confident.

Your thoughts matter.

Be proud of yourself.

You do not need to be perfect.

You are loved.

You belong.

You can reach your goals.

Stand up for yourself.

Anything you dream can be possible.

You can either tear girls down or build them up with your words. You can allow others to say things that are harmful to girls' self-esteem, or you can demonstrate positive communication and encouragement. You can remain silent, or you can advocate.

For example, my (Adam) daughter, Greta, is the older of my two children and seems to be the more natural leader. In fact we found out someone at her school called her "bossy." Her brother also tried to say she was bossy, but instead of allowing this word to fester and potentially damage Greta's self-esteem, my wife and I stepped in quickly to talk through what leadership is and what it looks like, hoping to steer Greta toward these positive characteristics.

Think about the response you'd like to deliver if and when someone calls your daughter or another young female around you "bossy." While you may feel uneasy about stepping in to guide the conversation, failing to do so can have lasting negative effects. For example, if you hear someone scolding a girl for being bossy, consider saying: "Let's not use the word 'bossy' to describe people. Sarah was actually showing great leadership potential just now. To be completely honest, I'd like to congratulate her on how she approached the situation."

This response is subtle and has a much different outcome than a one-way conversation where someone is accused of being bossy, and it serves as a great teaching moment.

To be clear, there is also room in this conversation to talk with the child who was called "bossy" to ensure she is choosing her words and manner appropriately. My wife and I have had conversations with our daughter about how to approach a situation or how she could articulate her message in a different way. Kids, especially those with stronger personalities, don't know how to navigate these conversations unless you coach them.

Take advantage of these "teachable moment" situations. Remaining silent when girls are disparaged is one of the most detrimental things an adult can do. Remember, your words are powerful and can have a lasting impact on girls, so be positive and encouraging. And make it your priority to speak up for girls, advocate for them, step in when needed to correct inappropriate behavior, and stand next to, in front of, or behind a girl who needs some support.

> **Remaining silent when girls are disparaged is one of the most detrimental things an adult can do.**

How we talk to girls, about girls, and around girls sets the tone for them and others in their lives. Stop laughing at disrespectful jokes and comments. Speak up when you hear something degrading. Be positive, appropriate, and encouraging. Remember, your words last a lifetime, so choose them carefully!

A CALL TO ACTION

★ Think about a time when you heard someone talk in a negative way to another person. Did you say something in response, or were you silent? If you responded, what did you say? If you were silent, what would you say next time?

★ Make a list of three to five positive phrases to use with girls and work intentionally to incorporate these into your daily speech.

CHAPTER 25

Surround Girls with Positive People

OUR GIRLS ARE A direct reflection of the people around them. Surrounding girls with the right people can and will make a positive difference. It's important they're surrounded by people who will help them aim higher, go bigger and farther, and make positive decisions.

I (Adam) can already see this is true with my daughter. Certain people bring out the best in her, and others do not. I've coached her soccer team for the past two years, and it's amazing to see her—and all her teammates—flourish in this environment. I realize not everyone is an athlete or wants to play team sports, but this soccer team has provided a tremendous atmosphere for these girls. During practice they're working together, and we coaches are pushing their limits to see how they can improve individually and as a team. One girl will try a new type of pass or kick, and then everyone will do the same. They'll "one up" one another, but do so in an encouraging and positive way.

This is the type of situation I want my daughter to be in, and these are the type of people I want to surround my daughter with. These are the girls who will make her better, the girls who will encourage her to make positive decisions. This is the group that will help instill in her a work ethic to last a lifetime. And this is the field, where she plays soccer and is learning so many valuable lessons, that we want her to be on so she can reach her full potential.

As you think about your own girls, strongly consider surrounding them with:

- positive role models
- courageous personalities
- a diverse set of friends from all different backgrounds
- others you would be proud to call your own
- humor and laughter
- opportunities you didn't have, so they are exposed to different experiences
- people who will encourage them
- people who lift them up
- people who love them
- people who will cheer them up
- men who show them respect
- artistic opportunities
- opportunities to be healthy
- encouragers
- dreamers
- truth
- experiences to build them up
- family, so they know the value and importance of it
- girls who want to be their friend

Your girls are a direct reflection of you and the other people with whom they spend the most time.

Your girls are a direct reflection of you and the other people with whom they spend the most time. While they will figure this out through their life experiences, as their adults, you must guide and encourage them in the right direction.

A CALL TO ACTION

★ What characteristics do you most want the girls in your life to possess? How can you proactively put your girls in contact with people who possess these characteristics?

★ How can you more effectively model these characteristics personally?

CHAPTER 26

Be a "World-Changer"

From Erin Jones, educator, speaker

AN ENCOURAGING WORD FROM a trusted mentor or an admired adult can make a lasting impact on a young girl. Or, as in my case, it may even convince her she can change the world!

In 1979 I was a fourth grader attending the American School of The Hague where my parents taught. My best friend was Yael Ronan, the daughter of the Israeli ambassador to the United Nations. Although I was raised a Protestant, I was drawn to Yael's Jewish culture, family, and faith. I found something special about the Jewish community and the Hebrew language. I read every book I could find by and about Jewish people. I wanted to attend Yeshiva (even though it was a school for Jewish students), and I wanted to live on a kibbutz.

I was also moved by what Yael had to endure in 1979. Her country was at war with Palestine. Regularly, bombs went off in Israel, guns were shot, and lives were lost. Because this was before the internet or the current simplicity of international phone calls, Yael often arrived at school teary-eyed, anxious, and wondering if all of her family members were still alive.

As our friendship developed, an idea formed in my head: What if I could solve the Middle East crisis? What if I could bring peace to the region? I was determined to become a bridge, to be part of the solution. Yes, I was only nine years old, but I already spoke English and Dutch fluently. Adding Hebrew and Arabic seemed like a natural first step toward building a bridge between these nations. So I began to learn. Every day I ate lunch, either with Yael to learn Hebrew or with another friend, Najat from Libya, who helped me learn Arabic.

In December we were informed the wife of Egyptian President Anwar Sadat would be visiting our school to talk about peace. Her country was in the middle of a civil war at the time. In fact, her husband would be assassinated almost one year later.

I was selected as one of three fourth-grade children to present their ideas for world peace to President Sadat's wife. I knew exactly what my plan was, and I invested hours preparing a beautiful poster to convey it. On the day of her visit, President Sadat's wife shared a brief message and then invited the selected students to have lunch with her. As we pulled out our posters for our presentations, I noticed immediately the other two had professional photos attached and typed words, while mine had been crafted with a new box of crayons and my fourth-grade penmanship and artistic ability. Suddenly, I was absolutely ashamed and utterly embarrassed by my work.

When President Sadat's wife asked, "So children, how are you going to change the world?" there was silence for a moment. How could I have thought my childish project was worthy of presentation to a president's wife? But suddenly, I realized that although my poster may have looked childish, its content represented true passion—true motivation to change the world in significant ways. Instead of wallowing in self-doubt, I broke the silence:

"I am going to solve the Middle East crisis. I am going to bring peace to the Middle East."

I began to describe all I had drawn on my poster: the Arabic, Hebrew, and my friendship with Yael, driving me to want to make a difference in this particular part of the world.

As soon as I finished speaking, encouraging words poured from President Sadat's wife. She looked me right in the eye, pointed her finger at me, and called me by name. "Erin," she said, "You are a world-changer!" She was so convincing; I knew she meant it.

> She looked me right in the eye, pointed her finger at me, and called me by name. "Erin," she said, "You are a world-changer!" She was so convincing; I knew she meant it.

As soon as I returned to my classroom, I rushed to inform my teacher. "Mrs. Parlier, President Sadat's wife told me I am a world-changer. What do I need to do now?"

Without batting an eyelash, Mrs. Parlier reached into her desk drawer and pulled out a fifty-page packet of fractions. I was so eager to change the world I did all fifty pages that evening! I was convinced the path to my desired future was through fractions.

The next day, I handed my completed packet to her and asked. "Mrs. Parlier, what do I need to do now?" After looking through the packet, shocked I had stayed up all night to finish them, she reached into her desk drawer and pulled out another packet of fractions. I completed close to one hundred of those packets during the year. I was so determined to change the world, I was willing to do whatever was asked of me.

I realize now—almost forty years later, twenty-five of those as a teacher—changing the world requires more than being able to do math problems. But this experience taught me how much power encouraging and affirming words had on my passion. President Sadat's wife's words changed me and convinced me I could be a world-changer. Mrs. Parlier fed my passion further, teaching me that greatness requires going beyond simply what is expected in order to invest in my *best* self.

Educators and leaders, your words matter. Choose to speak life and inspiration into your children. Be a world-changer by changing their worlds!

A CALL TO ACTION

★ What are some encouraging words others spoke to you when you were a child? How did they positively impact you?

★ How can you specifically speak encouragement into the lives of the girls you work with?

CHAPTER 27

Nudge Girls to Discover Their Voices

From Todd Schmidt, principal

ONE OF MY GREATEST challenges as an educator and a parent is helping my students—and especially my own children—embrace risk-taking and jump into the unknown. While it is hardly surprising children are averse to taking chances, they need to understand that, even if they fail or struggle, risk-taking is a mark of success and confidence.

My eldest daughter loves to sing—I mean *really* loves to sing! Come into my house, and she is belting out a tune, anything from Broadway to Taylor Swift. When our family gets together for holidays, you can be sure we will have some sort of singing performance. She also shares my penchant for loud, exuberant singing in the car, though she is *far* more talented than her tone-deaf father!

When she joined the choir in middle school, she seemed content to be one of the many voices in the background. She appeared resolute about not standing out in any way. While she had raw talent, it quickly became apparent she had a lot of doubts about her abilities. Even though family members complimented her singing, in her mind she was not as good as others in the choir.

My wife and I discussed ways to help build her self-confidence and signed her up for voice lessons; however, we practically had to drag her kicking and screaming to her first lesson. Despite her protests and tears as she walked to the door, she left the first voice lesson with a smile on her face and a song in her heart! In the following weeks and months, we watched excitedly as she gained confidence, skills, and techniques. All these culminated in her having the courage to stand up and perform with other voice students in front of their families. I learned an important lesson during this time: Parents have to nudge their children out of their comfort zones every once in a while.

Despite these early successes, my daughter still doubted whether she was good enough to try out for solos or the more advanced school choir. She experienced a turning point when her choir teacher used the final exam as part of the audition process for next year. After my daughter finished her piece, her teacher looked at her, stunned, and asked, "Where has this voice been?" While this was definitely a boost to her confidence, she still felt unsure of her skill, and she avoided auditioning for the show choir, claiming her parents would not be able to get her to rehearsals! When my daughter shared this with me later, I asked why she didn't want to audition, and she confided she wasn't sure she had the skill set of the other singers and was fearful of not being successful.

> I assured her my primary desire was for her simply to try. I didn't care whether or not she got a solo; I just wanted her to audition.

At this point, I realized our children not only need to be encouraged to take risks, but they also need to know the adults in their lives are close by to support them or pick them up if they fall. I assured her my primary desire was for her simply to try. I didn't care whether or not she got a solo; I just wanted her to audition.

One of the most gratifying days for me as a parent was when my daughter got her first solo. One of the most challenging days was when she didn't get a part. On both occasions, I told her I was proud of her for taking a risk. My wife and I also strove to avoid the "overs"—over-celebrating when she triumphed or over-wallowing when she missed the mark. Instead we talked about humility when she got the part and perseverance when she didn't.

My daughter's willingness to take risks is still a work in progress, but I sincerely hope she and my other daughters will learn the value and importance of taking a risk, facing the uncertainty, and trying again when things don't work out the way they had hoped. Ultimately, I want them to know I am always their biggest cheerleader, standing beside them and never giving up on them!

A CALL TO ACTION

★ How can you encourage your girls to take risks and embrace opportunities?

★ How can you create a safer space for the girls you work with to take risks?

CHAPTER 28

Teach Them They Are Valuable

OVER AND OVER, **I** (Lynmara) see young girls and older women struggle to define who they are and allow others to determine their worth. I'm saddened to know so many girls give others the power to tell them how valuable they are—power which is often misused. Girls allow those they have relationships with to make them feel scared, sad, and worthless. If adults are not intentional about raising confident girls who are fearless as they step out into the world, I am afraid they will continue to allow partners to mistreat them and society to convince them their bodies are not perfect. Their hearts will become empty, waiting for another person to fill them up. Showering them with love and affirmations can become the antidote to others' low expectations, allowing us to build strong ladies who know how much they are worth.

I struggled with this—battling to believe what my heart knew was right when society was telling me something else was better. Often I looked to peers for advice, but they knew as little as I did about what love and respect should look like. While I had a wonderful family, some important conversations never took place, leaving me without the necessary skills to stand up for myself when I went out into the world. As many girls do, I created a narrative in my head of fairy tales and perfection, forgetting my worth was so much more. And when those Prince Charmings disappointed me, I was left not knowing what to do. For years I made excuses for others' behaviors and made *myself* the one responsible for how I had been treated.

If adults are not intentional about teaching our girls how they deserve to be treated, someone else could—and likely will—set those expectations for them. Never be afraid to be honest with your children about the dangers and disappointments in life. Prepare them to set boundaries, be courageous, and say *no* when needed. While you cannot be with them at all times, the words you give them now will come back to your kids when they face adversity.

> If adults are not intentional about teaching our girls how they deserve to be treated, someone else could—and likely will—set those expectations for them.

Teach your girls their worth does *not* come from others. Teach them they are beautiful, amazing human beings, and anyone who says differently simply does not deserve to share space with them. Emphasize they do not need to be in abusive relationships, compromise their values, hurt themselves, or take disrespect from anyone. Teach them they can stand up, make a choice, and be amazing, and that those they let into their lives should *add* value, not take it away. And for any who might suggest that self-reliance and control are negative traits, promoting a woman's quest for these is not about independence but rather self-worth. It is not about power, it's about strength. It is not about feminism, but about having the courage to stand in our truth.

I can't help thinking about my own daughters and the example I have given them all these years. In everything you do, teach your children about love, expectations, respect, how to be kind, and how to live in a seemingly broken world. I hope you can be a light and inspire girls around you to stand up and be comfortable in their own skin. Rally around other girls to lift them up and remind them of their worth.

Women and girls must understand they have been fearfully and wonderfully made. Your purpose is to compliment others, but you can't complete them; they must do this on their own. They are in control of their own happiness. Teach your girls never to rely on another person to make them happy or feel loved. Instill in them a belief that they are enough and possess the skills to go after their dreams and make an impact in this world. Tell your girls how beautiful and amazing they are. Tell them to look in the mirror and know they deserve the very best.

A CALL TO ACTION

★ How can you be intentional about teaching girls their true worth?

★ Leave a note for someone telling them how amazing they are.

CHAPTER 29

Support Them through Recognition

ONE OF THE MOST valuable lessons I (Lynmara) have learned in my life is people *do* eventually recognize others, even if it takes a long time! Prior to the spring of 2017, though, I hadn't learned this. I had been clinging to a narrative I'd learned early as a child: everything happening to me was only a matter of luck and was not the result of anyone watching or supporting me in some way.

But my narrative changed when I scrolled through my work email early in 2017 and noticed a subject line reading, "National School Board Association's 20 to Watch." Figuring it was another informational email or an invitation to nominate someone, I opened it casually. However, as I read it, I learned *I* had been selected as one of the recipients of the "NSBA's 20 to Watch" award for 2017! Me?! I stopped and read it again. Surely this can't be true; I was positive it was a mistake.

After reading it multiple times, I was convinced it was *my* name on the email. And there was another name also: Adam Welcome. Adam had nominated me for the award! I'd had no idea. Adam and I had met a year before, when he visited our school while in the DC area, and now he had taken the time to nominate me. I was in awe, and I cried. His gesture proved the saying true, "Do everything with excellence. You never know who is watching."

Overwhelmed by his nomination and generosity, I was also humbled he took note of what we were doing at our school and had compiled a beautiful summary for the nomination packet. He had let the world know my work mattered. A *man* had lifted me up and reminded me I was deserving of recognition. He did not have to do it, but he did.

I struggled a bit to receive the recognition. I would have never personally highlighted our work for fear of being perceived as "pretentious" or "self-promoting." Society says women who take this initiative are not "classy" and could be seen as "too strong." Confidence in females is a turn off for many; in fact, women are often trained not to share too much for fear of coming across the wrong way. For years I had been trained to put the spotlight on others. Silence, however, does not equal humility. Adam reminded me that being humble can be beautiful, but it should never hide the excellent work my school is doing with kids. He showed me I could be humble but still share my voice with others.

> **Society says women who take this initiative are not "classy" and could be seen as "too strong."**

I'm thankful for Adam and other great men who have pushed me to be a better leader, given me advice, and encouraged me to pursue my dreams. Working together and supporting each other in this way is invaluable to our goal of making our schools—and this world—a better place.

When Adam and I decided to write this book, I experienced another *this does not happen to people like me* moments. I was honest with Adam and told him, "I am overwhelmed in a happy way—I feel like crying." When he responded with, "It is okay to cry, Lynmara," I was touched—and I did cry. It was a beautiful moment because he saw my tears, not as a sign of weakness, but as an expression of appreciation. He allowed me to be vulnerable and express my excitement in a way others would have perceived as weakness.

Girls need to understand that some boys will be their best friends and will be okay with them crying. Those cheering us will even wear a tutu just to see a girl smile (Thank you, Adam!). Those boys will be girls' biggest cheerleaders, mentors, and the ones who will challenge girls to pursue their dreams. These are the boys that girls need to share their voices with. They need to invite them into powerful conversations that will initiate change in the world. Together they will change the narrative and see that the fruit of a fight for equality is well worth the effort.

Begin the movement. Be an Adam Welcome to the girls in your life.

A CALL TO ACTION

★ Discuss with a group of male and female colleagues how you can support one another.

★ Be intentional about celebrating others and recognizing their achievements.

CONCLUSION

WE HOPE THIS BOOK has caused you to think. We hope it has opened your eyes to the girls in your life—how they're spoken to, treated, included, or excluded. We hope it has made you more aware of anything that might rob them of opportunity in their lives.

Many of the changes you can make are small and subtle, but you can have a profound and lasting impact on the life of a girl and her place in the world. Society has not made girls a priority, and you must change this. Please join the conversation to empower girls so they have *every* opportunity to achieve their full potential.

What can you do to empower the girls in your world? For starters, consider these ideas from Erin Jones:

- Recognize your girls will never be perfect. Allow them grace to make mistakes. Assure them they will make some bad choices, but encourage them to forgive themselves, apologize when necessary, and get back up! If you're a parent, allow your daughter to fail while she still lives under your roof, as mistakes and missteps are incredible learning opportunities. Only "rescue" your daughter when she has put herself in physical or emotional danger. Allow her to learn how to fall down and get back up.

- Be patient. No matter how much potential a girl has, she will not always meet your expectations and your timetable. Stay the course with her.
- If you're a parent and your daughter has an interest in something you find frivolous or not of interest, invest in it anyway. Do not expect your daughter to live out your dreams. Empower her to accomplish whatever dreams *she* desires.
- Point out to each girl her own kind of beautiful. Remind her that part of what makes her beautiful is the fact that she is the only one who looks like she does.
- Encourage girls to find what they are good at and to be willing to put in extra effort to be *great* at something. Encourage them to keep trying new things until they find "their" talent.
- Instill in girls the importance of surrounding themselves with great people by choosing friends wisely and hanging out with people who are smarter, faster, and stronger than they are so they're always motivated to be their best.
- Inspire girls to be in charge of their own lives and never give power to other people or allow others to tell their stories for them.

While these are a few fantastic ideas, there is so much you can do to change the current narrative. You can create conditions in which girls can become strong individuals who are fearless to step into the world and be amazing. You can intentionally set a course where equality reigns and all can operate out of their gifts, regardless of their gender.

If you identify with any of these stories, please know there is hope. Do not miss an opportunity to take a seat at the table and challenge the status quo. Your young generation needs you. The battle to empower girls is one we must all take part in. They deserve to be the best they can be.

BIBLIOGRAPHY

"Our accelerated approach to diversity and inclusion." Google Diversity. https://diversity.google/#tab=tech.

Sax, Linda J., Kathleen J. Lehman, Jerry A. Jacobs, Allison Kanny, Gloria Lim, Laura Paulson, and Hilary B. Zimmerman. "Anatomy of an Enduring Gender Gap: The Evolution of Women's Participation in Computer Science." *The Journal of Higher Education* 88, no. 2 (2016): 258-293. doi: 10.1080/00221546.2016.1257306.

Koh, Yoree. "Twitter's Diversity Report: Women Make Up 30% of Workforce." *The Wall Street Journal.* July 23, 2014. https://blogs.wsj.com/digits/2014/07/23/twitters-diversity-report-women-make-up-30-of-workforce.

Michael Jr. "Know Your Why." YouTube video, 3:49. Posted by Michael Jr., January 8, 2017. https://www.youtube.com/watch?v=1ytFB8TrkTo.

Robnett, Paige. "How Women and Girls Are Marching Toward Equity in Sports." *AAUW.* March 16, 2016. https://www.aauw.org/2016/03/16/women-in-sports.

Williams, Maxine. "Building a More Diverse Facebook." *Facebook Newsroom.* Press Release, June 25, 2014. https://newsroom.fb.com/news/2014/06/building-a-more-diverse-facebook.

MORE FROM

DAVE BURGESS Consulting, Inc.

Since 2012, DBCI has been publishing books that inspire and equip educators to be their best. For more information on our DBCI titles or to purchase bulk orders for your school, district, or book study, visit DaveBurgessConsulting.com/DBCIbooks.

More from the PIRATE™ Series

Teach Like a PIRATE by Dave Burgess
eXPlore Like a Pirate by Michael Matera
Learn Like a Pirate by Paul Solarz
Play Like a Pirate by Quinn Rollins
Run Like a Pirate by Adam Welcome

Lead Like a PIRATE™ Series

Lead Like a PIRATE by Shelley Burgess and Beth Houf
Balance Like a Pirate by Jessica Cabeen, Jessica Johnson, and Sarah Johnson
Lead beyond Your Title by Nili Bartley
Lead with Culture by Jay Billy
Lead with Literacy by Mandy Ellis

Leadership & School Culture

Culturize by Jimmy Casas

Escaping the School Leader's Dunk Tank by Rebecca Coda and Rick Jetter

From Teacher to Leader by Starr Sackstein

The Innovator's Mindset by George Couros

Kids Deserve It! by Todd Nesloney and Adam Welcome

Let Them Speak by Rebecca Coda and Rick Jetter

The Limitless School by Abe Hege and Adam Dovico

The Pepper Effect by Sean Gaillard

The Principled Principal by Jeffrey Zoul and Anthony McConnell

The Secret Solution by Todd Whitaker, Sam Miller, and Ryan Donlan

Start. Right. Now. by Todd Whitaker, Jeffrey Zoul, and Jimmy Casas

Stop. Right. Now. by Jimmy Casas and Jeffrey Zoul

Unmapped Potential by Julie Hasson and Missy Lennard

They Call Me "Mr. De" by Frank DeAngelis

Your School Rocks by Ryan McLane and Eric Lowe

Technology & Tools

50 Things You Can Do with Google Classroom by Alice Keeler and Libbi Miller

50 Things to Go Further with Google Classroom by Alice Keeler and Libbi Miller

140 Twitter Tips for Educators by Brad Currie, Billy Krakower, and Scott Rocco

Block Breaker by Brian Aspinall

Code Breaker by Brian Aspinall

Google Apps for Littles by Christine Pinto and Alice Keeler

Master the Media by Julie Smith

Shake Up Learning by Kasey Bell

Social LEADia by Jennifer Casa-Todd

Teaching Math with Google Apps by Alice Keeler and Diana Herrington

Teaching Methods & Materials

All 4s and 5s by Andrew Sharos

Ditch That Homework by Matt Miller and Alice Keeler

Ditch That Textbook by Matt Miller

Educated by Design by Michael Cohen, The Tech Rabbi

The EduProtocol Field Guide by Marlena Hebern and Jon Corippo

Instant Relevance by Denis Sheeran

LAUNCH by John Spencer and A.J. Juliani

Make Learning MAGICAL by Tisha Richmond

Pure Genius by Don Wettrick

Shift This! by Joy Kirr

Spark Learning by Ramsey Musallam

Sparks in the Dark by Travis Crowder and Todd Nesloney

Table Talk Math by John Stevens

TeachingLand by Amanda Fox and Mary Ellen Weeks

Tech with Heart by Stacey Roshan

The Classroom Chef by John Stevens and Matt Vaudrey

The Wild Card by Hope and Wade King

The Writing on the Classroom Wall by Steve Wyborney

Inspiration, Professional Growth & Personal Development

The Four O'Clock Faculty by Rich Czyz

Be REAL by Tara Martin

Be the One for Kids by Ryan Sheehy

Creatively Productive by Lisa Johnson

The EduNinja Mindset by Jennifer Burdis

How Much Water Do We Have? by Pete and Kris Nunweiler

P Is for Pirate by Dave and Shelley Burgess

A Passion for Kindness by Tamara Letter

The Path to Serendipity by Allyson Apsey

Sanctuaries by Dan Tricarico

Shattering the Perfect Teacher Myth by Aaron Hogan

Stories from Webb by Todd Nesloney

Talk to Me by Kim Bearden

The Zen Teacher by Dan Tricarico

Children's Books

Dolphins in Trees by Aaron Polansky

The Princes of Serendip by Allyson Apsey

ABOUT THE AUTHORS

Lynmara Colón brings the perspective of a teacher, assistant principal, and principal, positions she has held since becoming an educator in 2000.

As principal of Mary Williams Elementary School in 2014, she served over 1,100 students in kindergarten through fifth grade and increased reading engagement by leading a culture of literacy. She now heads the office providing comprehensive registration services to English learners and immigrant children, including translation and interpretation services, in a school division serving over 90,000 students. These students represent 124 countries and 149 languages.

Colón holds two master's degrees: one in curriculum and instruction and the other in educational leadership. She is currently pursuing her doctorate in education through Old Dominion University.

Find her online at leadwithmagic.com and principalcolon.edublogs.org, and on Twitter @TheColon_s.

Adam Welcome has been a teacher, assistant principal, principal, director of innovation and technology, and also travels around the country to speak and work with school districts and other organizations.

Adam was nominated for Technology Leader of the Year by *Tech & Learning* magazine in 2010 and was recognized as Principal of the Year in 2013. He was named the East Bay CUE Site Leader of the Year in 2016 and, most recently, was selected by the National School Board Association as a "20 to Watch" in the nation.

Adam is also the co-author/founder of *Kids Deserve It!* and the author of *Run Like a Pirate*. In his spare time, Adam runs on a daily basis, skis in Lake Tahoe with his family, and loves to travel the world.

Connect with Adam at mradamwelcome.com, on Twitter and Instagram @mradamwelcome and if you need a speaker for your district, conference, or event, contact Adam directly at adamwelcome@gmail.com.

CPSIA information can be obtained
at www.ICGtesting.com
Printed in the USA
BVHW040220300519
549671BV00017B/307/P

BARNES&NOBLE.com

www.bn.com

Sold To:
Debra Faulhefer
6513 Charles Ct
MACUNGIE, PA
18062
United States of America

Ship To:
Debra Faulhefer
6513 Charles Ct
MACUNGIE, PA
18062
United States of America

Customer Service:
1 800 THE BOOK
http://help.barnesandnoble.com

Order #: 407975/216   **PO#:** 407975/216

Shipping Method:
UM / B&N.COM

Order Date: 05/30/19

Qty	Description	Item #	Our Price	Total
1	Empower Our Girls: Opening the	9781949595369	16.91	16.91

Please note: PA state sales tax was collected on this order.

Merchandise Total: $16.91
Tax Amount: $1.02
Shipment Total: $17.93

If you are not satisfied with your order, you may return it within 30 days of the delivery date (14 days for Nook devices and accessories). For your convenience, items may be returned to the address on the packing slip or returned to your local Barnes & Noble store (check the local store refund policy for details). Postage is not refundable.

Choose a return reason below and include this slip with the item in your package. Please cut out label on the dotted line and affix to carton being returned.

☐ Wrong Quantity
☐ Defective or Damaged in Transit
☐ Wrong Merchandise Received
☐ Other (please explain)

Pay Method: PP
Credit Card #: 735N

From:
Debra Faulhefer
6513 Charles Ct
MACUNGIE, PA
18062
United States of America

Order #:
407975/216

To:
BARNES AND NOBLE.COM
RETURNS CENTER
1 BARNES AND NOBLE WAY
MONROE TOWNSHIP
NJ 08831 341/

0000038808486547172

WC 207 #7DLW4 20K2901 05/30/19 3363549S

D150-09020Y03